THE ESSENTIALS OF THEISM

THE ESSENTIALS OF THEISM

by

D. J. B. HAWKINS

GREENWOOD PRESS, PUBLISHERS
WESTPORT, CONNECTICUT

The Library of Congress has catalogued this publication as follows:

Library of Congress Cataloging in Publication Data

Hawkins, Denis John Bernard, 1906-1964.
    The essentials of theism.

    1. Theism. I. Title.
BL200.H38 1973   211'.3   72-9373
ISBN 0-8371-6579-2

Originally published in 1950 by Sheed and Ward,
New York

Reprinted with the permission of Sheed & Ward, Inc.

Reprinted in 1973 by Greenwood Press,
a division of Congressional Information Service, Inc.
88 Post Road West, Westport, Connecticut 06881

Library of Congress catalog card number 72-9373
ISBN 0-8371-6579-2

Printed in the United States of America

10 9 8 7 6 5 4 3 2

CONTENTS

THE ESSENTIALS OF THEISM

CHAPTER I

INTRODUCTION

I

A BOOK in which the existence and nature of God are discussed by a process of abstract philosophical analysis and reasoning needs in the circumstances of today a longer introduction than it would have needed in the past. At most periods of the history of European thought such a discussion would have seemed a necessary part of the duty of any philosopher. Nowadays, a great number of philosophers who would appear otherwise to have but few certainties are at any rate insistent that they have nothing to offer on this subject. A widespread distrust of reason makes many of those who desire to treat the subject resort to an argument from religious and mystical experience rather than to metaphysics. We must begin by explaining why we think that philosophy has something to say about God, and why we still have recourse to the method of metaphysical reasoning which Kant is generally supposed to have overturned.

In the first place we must point out why we are not induced to renounce our project at the outset on account of any of the various modern attempts to explain religion away, whether in anthropological, psychological or sociological terms or on any other basis that might be conceived. Animism or ancestor-worship or whatever the hypothesis may be, we are told how primitive man, not a little lower than the angels but only a little higher than the brutes, with a half-awakened intelligence and an infinite capacity for jumping to conclusions, persuaded himself that his life and fortune depended upon supernatural beings or gods, and that from these first crude gods came, by a process of refinement, the monotheism which until lately was the creed of Western man. Alternatively we are told that the notion of God is an enlarged Father-imago endowed with the qualities which the Super-ego proposes to our admiration and imitation. It is still more vociferously proclaimed that religion " is nothing but the fantastic reflection in men's minds of those external forces which control their daily life, a reflection in which the terrestrial forces assume the form of supernatural forces."[1] Hence, as man by means of physical science gains control over his environment, this fantastic reflection will lose its power and fade away.

We do not propose to attack these ingenious theories of religion on their own ground, for there is no need to do so. We are not convinced by them, because they presuppose that there is no rational basis for a belief in God. Evidently, then, we must first examine whether such a rational basis for theism exists. If God does exist, the origin of religion has to be explained primarily by a recognition of his existence, however crudely expressed and however mingled with anthropomorphic and mythological elements. Only if it turned out that the rational basis of religion was inadequate, would it be worth while to consider how men might have been misled into making erroneous affirmations about it.

The philosopher, therefore, cannot abdicate his traditional

[1] Engels: *Anti-Dühring*, part III, ch. 5.

task of inquiring into the rational basis of religion. Religion is a great and enduring fact in human history, and, if it has sometimes been the source of evils, religious wars and persecutions, human sacrifices and consecrated immoralities, nevertheless it has also been the source of nearly all that is best in the story of mankind. When we think what religion has meant in the way of insight and activity in its saints and heroes, we must admit a high antecedent probability that the occasional evils engendered by religion have been a perversion and that the religious impulse is an indispensable value in human life. And, if it is a value, this can only be because it is a response to reality; there can be no profound and permanent value in self-deception, even if its immediate effects happen to be salutary. The least religious epochs have been periods of fatigued civilization like our own, but even in our own period religion is alive. Even in an epoch like our own, a thinker can scarcely claim to be a philosopher if he leaves so momentous a feature of human life out of account or merely attempts to explain it away.

A difficulty arises, however, when we remember that the historical religions have usually presented themselves as divine revelations, as messages from God to man delivered at a definite point in time. Inquiry into the occurrence and contents of a divine revelation is outside the scope of philosophy; it is the proper task of the theologian. Yet more general questions about the existence and nature of a divine being, which have no historical aspect, remain within the province of the philosopher. Logically, indeed, such questions are presupposed by theological discussion; we must know that God exists before we can judge that he has revealed himself. Christianity, at any rate, has never regarded the fundamental recognition of God as being due solely to Christianity itself, and St. Paul in the beginning could confidently appeal to the Athenians to admit that God was not far from each one of us, for in him we live and move and have our being. The philosopher, therefore, while not trespassing upon revealed theology, has his own proper task to perform in exploring the possibility and mode of a natural knowledge of God based on universal principles of reason.

Here, of course, the philosopher, if he happens to be a Christian, will be told that he is merely rationalizing a conviction previously embraced on other and logically less reputable grounds. Bertrand Russell objects that St. Thomas Aquinas's " appeal to reason is, in a sense, insincere, since the conclusion to be reached is fixed in advance."[1] But it is the condition of man to be a social animal even in his thinking, to be influenced by social tradition and environment, and to be indoctrinated as a child before he reflects as a man. It is equally his business, as his mind matures, to pass a reflective judgment on the influences which have moulded him and are still working upon him. Those who profess to think in complete independence are all the more inevitably subject to the intellectual influences of their times, because their declaration of self-sufficiency incapacitates them from acknowledging and, therefore, from criticizing the influences which bear upon them. The philosopher who has been educated as a Christian may, consequently, be given the benefit of a claim to honest reflection and to the acquisition of an honest philosophical conviction about some of the doctrines which he accepted before he approached philosophy. If we have been told that the Eiffel Tower exists at Paris and we see it with our own eyes when we go there, we do not think it necessary to suppose that we are suffering from an hallucination due to what we have been previously told.

[1] Bertrand Russell: *History of Western Philosophy*, bk. II, ch.13, p. 484.

2

This conception of a philosophical or natural theology, distinct from theology in the stricter sense of the word, which is the elaboration of the contents of divine revelation, was worked out systematically by the mediaeval philosophers. It is the procedure which we associate with thinkers such as St. Thomas Aquinas, St. Bonaventure and Duns Scotus. Nor, in modern times, did it easily cease to command the attention of philosophers. Descartes and Leibniz, and even Berkeley, were attempting in their different ways to provide a natural theology just as their mediaeval predecessors had done. It was first Hume's attack on the causal principle and then, still more, Kant's criticism of the traditional arguments which turned men's minds in other directions. Thereafter those who sought to establish the validity of religious belief looked for a line of thought which would avoid the objections of Hume and of Kant. While some have followed in Kant's footsteps by representing religion as a postulate of moral aspiration, others have placed more reliance upon the observed facts of religious experience. A metaphysical natural theology is now cultivated almost exclusively by those who consciously hark back to the mediaeval tradition.

It will not be out of place to state at once why we shall not rely upon considerations about religious experience, which, at any rate since the time of Schleiermacher, have played so great a part in the philosophy of religion. Such thinking has been by no means valueless. It has made important contributions to religious psychology and to what may be described as the phenomenology of religion, but the question which concerns us here is whether it can by itself provide an adequate basis for religious belief. We can scarcely return a favourable answer to this question.

The appeal to religious experience may be understood in more than one way. It may be understood as an exhortation to go and have religious experience. This is the method of the revivalist preacher, but in a slightly more refined form it might also be the method of a philosopher. In ordinary life, if a man doubted whether tables existed, you would point to one and say, "There is a table." A philosopher may require a little more convincing on the question of tables, but even the most sceptical philosopher would scarcely deny the legitimacy of an appeal to experience for the existence of, say, yellow sense-data. Similarly, if a man queries the existence of acts of thinking, you can in the last resort only tell him to inspect the contents of consciousness and find them there; any reasoning which might be employed would be rather concerned with the removal of obstacles to this direct apprehension. So an empirical religious philosopher might ask his hearer to inspect his experience under certain conditions and to find God there.

Such an invitation, however, opens a door wide to self-deception and, as St. Thomas Aquinas remarked in another connection, merely invites the derision of the infidels. So many ambiguous states have been described as instances of religious experience. Recently someone has described how he was converted by listening to Beethoven, but it is still not clear whether by listening to Beethoven one can be converted to anything except Beethoven.[1] Emotional conversions may easily be followed by emotional reactions, and it does not appear that either the conversion or the reaction possesses genuine evidential value.

Of course the influence of beautiful words and exquisite music in religious worship, and even, on occasion, of ceremonial trappings and incense, may provoke emotions

[1] Cf. Warner Allen: *The Timeless Moment.*

which sentimental minds rashly identify as religious experiences. Even the sceptic is not exempt from such emotions, and, if the sceptic is Walter Pater in the chapel of Brasenose, the emotions are very refined indeed. But they are not obviously different from the emotions produced by music and poetry on more secular occasions, and in less cultivated minds they may not be very different from the emotional states aroused by crooners and dance-bands. A serious thinker will not indeed despise religious symbolism, but he will first want to convince himself that there is something to be symbolized by it. The point seems to be that genuine religious experience is a flowering consequent upon the long cultivation of the spiritual life in dry places and presupposing a prosaic rational conviction that God exists. Hence there is no available short cut to a purely empirical source of religious belief.

If, therefore, we cannot rely upon the appeal to religious experience understood as an exhortation to convince oneself by experiment, we have still to consider it when it is intended as a reference to the evidential value of the religious experiences of others. The reference might be either to the extraordinary experiences of mystics or to the ordinary spiritual life of the average devout believer. Mystical experience certainly deserves to be treated with respect. The honest sceptic can scarcely read the testimony of, say, St. John of the Cross, without suspecting that he had arrived at something real, and indeed at something more fully real than the objects of ordinary awareness. The difficulty would be to decide from the accounts of the mystics alone at what precisely they had arrived. St. John of the Cross, if we may recur to him, interpreted his experiences in concepts derived from the theology which he had studied, but it would be exceedingly difficult to convince anyone who had no independent belief in the validity of this theology that it provided the only possible interpretation of the saint's experiences.

What happens to mystics is often obscure to themselves, and, even when they have experiences which are dazzlingly bright to them, these are so dazzlingly bright that they can scarcely be expressed in human language. This is no objection to the validity of mysticism. If the mystics really have some direct awareness of an unique object in its uniqueness, this is precisely what we should expect; it is not to be supposed that they could do more than stammer about it. Nevertheless this is an objection to taking their experiences as the sole basis of ordinary religious belief. If we had no more to go upon, we might indeed be sure that there were more things, at least in heaven, than were dreamed of in our philosophy, but we should find it extremely difficult to be sure what these things were.

Finally we might think of the argument from religious experience as being an appeal to the facts of the spiritual life as exemplified in the ordinary devout believer. As we have already noted, religion is an impressive historical fact and, as such, must, to an unprejudiced mind, yield an antecedent probability that there is something in it. But we cannot be content simply to take in one another's intellectual washing. If there is something in religion, we want to know how to arrive at it on our own part; we want to know the intellectual character, and consequently the logical value, of the route by which men arrive at their religious beliefs. Now a direct experience of God seems to be a prerogative of extraordinary mystical states; even if mystical graces are more widely distributed than has sometimes been supposed, which may well be true, they seem always to follow upon a non-mystical spiritual life in which the knowledge of God is not direct.

But a knowledge which is not direct is inferential. It appears, therefore, that we shall be faithful to the facts of religion if we look for its possible justification in a plain and honest process of reasoning. Nevertheless an inferential interpretation of ordinary religious belief has difficulties of its own which must be overcome before entering upon it in detail.

3

It might easily be admitted that an ordinary religious life does not seem to contain any direct experience of God until we face the difficulties of supposing that the average man's knowledge of God is inferential. Can we face without qualms the assertion that the devout churchgoer has performed a metaphysical demonstration which Kant scrupled to accept and which taxed even the intellect of Aquinas? The ancient tag about Scylla and Charybdis presents itself with regrettable importunity.

Perhaps, however, we have allowed ourselves to be obsessed by the notion of inference as it appears in abstract logic; a more psychological appreciation of inference as a process of mind may help to resolve our difficulties. Of course, when we are reasoning about abstractions, as in mathematics, the procedure can only be of the formal and abstract sort which is set out by logicians. But inference about concrete existent things is on many occasions evidently much more informal and spontaneous, and it is not less useful or valid inference for that. When we look at the sky before going out and then take an umbrella, we may not notice at all that we are performing a perfectly sound inference. Reasoning, then, may be either formal, abstract and deliberate, as described by logicians, or informal, concrete and spontaneous. The explicit inference of logic is in the first instance the result of a reflective analysis of the implicit inference of everyday life. When it has thus been obtained, it both serves as a test of the validity of implicit inferences and can find a new field of application in the abstract sciences. If we are to say that the common man's religious beliefs are inferential, we shall be attributing to him not a fully reflective logical process but a spontaneous course of reasoning which usually becomes partly reflective but whose validity is not wholly dependent upon the degree of explicit analysis to which it attains.

Understood in this way, an inferential view no longer seems unplausible. No doubt the common man's religious reasoning is usually stimulated by teaching, but the result will not be a blind faith in social tradition. The teaching, like all teaching that is worth while, will arouse an individual intellectual activity. When you tell a child that God made the world, you are already suggesting to him the process of thought by which he may see that the world is such that it does not exist of itself but had to be made by God. While minds differ enormously in their degree of clearness and articulateness, the religious philosopher will recognize the reality of implicit inference and will not make himself ridiculous by a kind of metaphysical snobbery which condemns any but formal and explicit reasoning.

So far, of course, this is merely a hypothesis about the nature of religious belief, and it has to be tested by the success or failure of our rational analysis. Already, however, it indicates the way in which we may conceive the construction of a natural theology. Our task is similar to many other parts of philosophy. When a philosopher undertakes, for example, an analysis of perception, he is dealing with a series of questions to some of which the common man has already given spontaneous answers. He finds that many·

apparently immediate perceptual judgments are in fact inferential, and he can tell his hearers how they come to make such judgments. His work is valuable not only as an analysis of previously unreflective processes of mind, but also as a means of discriminating the logical status of different kinds of perceptual judgment. So it is also with ethics. Morality is not a creation of the moral philosopher, but the moral philosopher analyses and assesses ethical notions. In the same way the philosopher who thinks about God is not offering an entirely new foundation for religious belief but is analysing and judging an already existent process of reasoning.

A fully mature mind could not be content without such an analysis of its beliefs. The urge is not different from the impulse to pass from common sense to scientific knowledge in any other department of thought. But it is evident that, even for a mature mind, belief in the existence of a concrete reality is the result of co-operation between spontaneous and explicit inference. Just as, when we reach truth in the theory of perception or in moral philosophy, we are inclined to say, in an easily resolved paradox, that this is both something new and something which we had already thought, and as the new kind of knowledge and the old reinforce each other and together constitute our concrete conviction, so is this situation reproduced when we make explicit our reasoning about God. That is why, when education and environment have either not stimulated or have suppressed spontaneous religious conviction, the demonstrations of philosophical theology are apt at first to seem somewhat in the air. Yet they are not useless to the sceptic, for, while spontaneous inference can blossom into rational analysis, so there can be a psychological movement in the reverse direction, and abstract inference can strike roots in the living mind.

We should note also that religion is not a passionless field of thought like pure mathematics. Wherever a truth has practical applications, and no truth has more widespread practical applications than the existence of God, the influence of the will in assent must be taken into account. A man cannot help seeing what he sees, but he can refuse to turn his eyes to see it, and he can turn his eyes away and refuse to look at it again. Hence we make no profession of providing proofs which no one can decline to accept; we merely claim to offer reasoning which is in itself logically demonstrative, and that should be enough.

4

What we are going to offer, then, is a line of thought of the usual philosophical kind, proceeding by means of analytic and deductive logic. Here we must pause once again to prepare our reception, since this way of knowledge is nowadays often misunderstood and neglected. From the time of the eighteenth-century Encyclopaedists onwards, the scientific myth has fastened itself ever more firmly upon the popular, and even upon the educated, mind. There is a general impression, albeit of a vague and unanalysed kind, and indeed incapable of standing the test of analysis, that the methods of the physical sciences are simply identical with the methods of scientific knowledge. Hence it is supposed that there are certain established scientific truths about the material world, together with a less systematic body of psychological knowledge, while everything else is a matter of mere opinion. The tough-minded renounce the formation of opinions on other subjects, while the more tender-hearted are content to indulge their emotional preferences. This appalling collapse of standards of thinking is especially evident in contemporary popular writing, but it has not left even philosophers unaffected.

Of course, the veriest tyro in the logic of science must realize at once that the methods of induction and hypothesis do not stand upon their own feet but, if they are to be justified, must be justified by principles of pure logic and metaphysics. While modern scientific methods are extremely fruitful in practice but can hardly claim to reach more than theoretical probability and approximation, complete precision and certainty belong rather to the philosophical method of analytic and deductive logic. The ordinary educated man will grasp the nature of philosophical method by what he knows of mathematics. When he follows a geometrical theorem, his mind is working in a field of pure abstraction, in which experience serves only as a jumping-off ground for his concepts and not as the source of his conclusions. It is because, in mathematics, the mind can perceive directly the relationship between abstractions that mathematical reasoning enjoys its precision and certainty. So it is with philosophical reasoning; the method of the philosopher is essentially the same as the method of the mathematician, although the philosopher is operating at a deeper level of abstraction, and he is often dealing, as in our present inquiry, with questions which are complicated by human passions. But, when a genuine philosophical conclusion is attained, it is precise, certain and exempt from the variability of less privileged types of thinking.

We do not flatter ourselves that all this will carry conviction at once. We are living, especially in England, in an intellectual atmosphere in which empiricism of the Humian type tends to be taken for granted. That means that people are extraordinarily reluctant to accept anything but facts of consciousness and, indeed, facts on the surface of consciousness. Even if they overcome this obstacle, they will still be predisposed to think that Kant's objections have made a metaphysical approach to God for ever impossible. Kant's objections will have to be considered in their place, but it may be well to suggest at once that their force has far too often been assumed without any independent examination of what precisely Kant attacked and what precisely was the value of what he had to say about it. At any rate, a philosophical doctrine of God which treats Kant without servility is not on that account to be dismissed as a piece of archaeology. Our treatment is offered frankly as a natural theology on the medieval model, proceeding on grounds of objective logic and metaphysics and asserting the existence of God as a hard fact to be acknowledged by reason without reference to emotions, aspirations or any support other than honest and accurate thinking.

CHAPTER II

THE CONTINGENCY OF HISTORY

I

RELIGION in general, in so far as it is reflective, finds the ultimate explanation of the universe in the controlling influence of superhuman mind or minds. Theism makes its intellectual appeal by claiming that a personal God provides the only finally satisfactory explanation of the world in which we live. Hence it is appropriate to begin by discussing what we mean by explanation.

While explanation is usually contrasted with description, it arises naturally out of description. We describe a thing by answering the question what it is. This is the work of analysis, and analysis begins to be explanatory when we perceive an order in the factors of which a thing is composed and in the attributes and activities which it displays, such that some presuppose others and some are wholly or partly consequent upon others. Just as an adequate description of anything involves considering its relations with other things, so the knowledge of relations becomes explanatory when we consider not merely the relations which a thing happens to have but those which it must have in order to be precisely what it is or even to be at all. This understanding is what we seek when we investigate the conditions of a thing's existence and mode of development.

There is no explanation without an order of dependence of one fact upon another or of one notion upon another. That which is to be explained has to be exhibited as contingent upon something which enjoys a relative necessity. Necessity and contingency have a twofold application, on the one hand to the realm of *essence*, and on the other to the realm of *existence*.

In the realm of essence, when our explanations remain in the abstract, we aim at revealing the simple elements of our more complex concepts and at showing how more specific generalizations follow from those which are wider. In a deductive science we want to get back to primitive generalizations which carry their evidence and necessity in themselves, and then to show how truths of detail follow from these. In the sciences of observation, experiment and hypothesis, where the subject-matter does not permit such complete intelligibility, we still seek the simplest possible generalizations from which the rest may be deduced, in the hope that the hypotheses upon which we hit may approximate to the principles whose validity we might perceive directly if the subject-matter were more intrinsically intelligible to us. In both cases our procedure is governed by the maxim that explanation is incomplete until it arrives at what is necessary in itself.

It would be a great mistake to conclude from this application of the notions of necessity and dependence in the realm of essence that they were exclusively applicable there, and had no analogous validity in the realm of existence. The explanation of a fact is equally a search for that which exists with a prior necessity to the fact which is to be explained, and upon which this fact is consequent. The logical order is not self-sufficient, for knowing is essentially relative to being; there would not be logical necessities and dependences unless there were necessities and dependences of fact. It is because this is true, and clearly true, that we spontaneously seek a causal explanation of fact, and that the difficulties about causation raised by Hume and others are not an invitation to abdicate this primary acknowledgment, but a stimulus to analyse the notion of cause more adequately. To this point, however, we shall evidently have to return later.

We should remark that it is by actually explaining things that we find that we are able to explain things. We do not first decide out of the blue that the universe must be intelligible, and then set about understanding it; rather we find in particular instances that we can understand something of it. We find that we can form general concepts which are verified in particular areas of space and at particular points of time, and that in fortunate cases we can perceive relationships between these concepts which afford a clue to the relationships of the things which verify them. Hence we know, at any rate, that the universe is not wholly absurd; it is partly intelligible, even to us, and we can cherish an ideal of perfect intelligibility to which we may hope distantly to approximate. If we can establish that the universe is the work of Absolute Mind and that being exists primarily in the form of Absolute Mind, we shall know that everything is intelligible in principle and is actually understood by Absolute Mind. But that is the end, and not the beginning, of our investigation.

Nor, in our present inquiry, do we have to postulate at the outset that we must be able to find a final explanation of everything and to arrive at something which is self-explanatory. It is enough if we do not exclude the possibility of this. We are going to ask whether the world of temporal and changing things requires an explanation as a whole, and of what sort this explanation has to be, but we do not need to suppose erroneously that we understand the world completely before we ask and, maybe, answer these questions. It is enough if the world of experience manifests

some characteristic or characteristics which we do understand and which will serve both as stimulus and as means
for the mind to spring to something outside it.

2

We must first face the opposition of those who decline to
look for anything more ultimate than the process of history
itself. They hold, explicitly or implicitly, that the world of
history, if it were seen in its full unity and coherence, would
be seen also to be sufficient to itself. If time and history are
what they seem to be, such theories must be philosophies of
becoming, assigning to change and becoming a primacy over
being.

By a philosophy of becoming we do not mean every
system which emphasizes the reality of time and history;
becoming is evidently a factor to be taken seriously into
account by any sound philosophy. Nor is every evolutionary
doctrine a philosophy of becoming, for it seems to be true
that different types of things have been instantiated at
different times in the history of the world, and this demands
an appropriate explanation. A philosophy of becoming in
the full sense of the phrase would be one which tends to
explain being in terms of becoming rather than becoming in
terms of being; it is a kind of philosophy in which change is
primarily real and the concept of being is an abstraction
from, and impoverishment of, the rushing stream of cosmic
process.

The few cryptic sayings of Heraclitus which have been
preserved justify us in regarding him, with his doctrine of
universal flux, as the ancestor of the philosophies of becoming. Plato in the *Theaetetus*, with one of his flashes of
shrewd irony, represents the Heraclitean theory as being,

whether recognized or not, at the bottom of the complacent subjectivism of Protagoras and his like. But it is in modern times, when there has been so great an expansion of detailed historical knowledge, that the tendency to regard history as sufficient to itself has gained full force. In the pioneering work of Vico the attempt to provide a philosophy of history is capable of fitting within a broader system, but with Hegel philosophy becomes submerged in history. Hegel construes history in intellectualistic terms as the development of the Idea, so that the absolute is essentially a result and, in fact, an always incomplete result; events do not so much proceed from the absolute as tend towards its unfolding. The Hegelian dialectic proved equally susceptible of a materialistic interpretation in the hands of Marx and Engels and their followers. Finally, Bergson's doctrine of the *élan vital* derives its inspiration from biology, and hypostatizes the notion of life with its restless development and constant perishing to be born anew. These theories, and others like them, have become part of the intellectual climate of our time.

It is true that none of these systems can be described on closer inspection as a mere philosophy of becoming. For Hegel, although only the cosmic process as a whole can properly be called true, and consequently truth is a bacchanalian revel in which no participant is sober, it is nevertheless, from another point of view, at the same time a state of complete and transparent calm. More prosaically and more intelligibly, the Hegelian dialectic is an attempt to explain change by principles which are independent of change. The same must be said of its Marxist counterpart, and in any case Marxism is perhaps more significantly materialistic than dialectical, for the social dialectic is intended to work itself out within a measurable period by the establishment of a classless society. Bergson again, as his mental development proceeded, and he was a true philosopher in so far as it never ceased with life, began to look for something outside history to satisfy his ultimate cravings for understanding.

One might be tempted to echo Plato's complaint and to allege that the disciples of the doctrine of flux are themselves in a state of flux, shifting their ground so frequently that we hardly know when we have them. It would be more pertinent to use these points as evidence that a mere philosophy of becoming is incapable of maintaining itself, and to invite the philosophers of history to follow more persistently the clues which they have themselves provided to a type of explanation which transcends history. At any rate they are not to be criticized for having sought principles and laws of historical development; this is evidently a legitimate, although elusive, object of philosophical inquiry. They are to be adversely criticized here in so far as they shift the emphasis from being to becoming and, explicitly or implicitly, look upon principles of becoming as affording the final element in the understanding of the universe.

3

Turning to the question in the abstract, we must first say that becoming has no meaning except in terms of being. Becoming can be understood only as the coming-to-be of something, or as the transition by which something becomes something else. A pure doctrine of flux abolishes itself, because there would be nothing which becomes, and consequently there could be no becoming. While being is intrinsically intelligible, becoming is unintelligible without reference to being, as coming from being and as leading to being.

One of the virtues of the Aristotelian analysis of change in terms of potentiality and actuality is that it is manifestly anchored to the notion of being. When a thing is merely possible, or when an existent thing is merely capable of a new activity or state, it is so far in a condition of not-being; when it comes to exist, or when it acquires this new activity or state, it enters into a condition of being. Change is a passage from not-being to being or from being to not-being; actuality is actual being, and potentiality is potentiality of being. Hence we shall say to the disciples of Heraclitus in every age that, while we applaud their inquiry into the principles of change and development, they must not think that they have completed the work of philosophy until they have risen above the flux and reduced becoming to the source of its intelligibility in being.

The interpretation of becoming in terms of being calls for the notion of causation in the sense of a temporal relation of antecedent and consequent. It is this meaning of causation which has received the greatest share of attention in modern times, but it is not the only meaning of causation. An agent as such is not the antecedent but the simultaneous source of its activity, and agency also deserves the name of cause. The temporal sense of causation cannot apply to God, for God certainly cannot be conceived as the first member of a temporal series. Hence a consideration of temporal causality cannot be an adequate approach to our present subject, but it has a certain function in a preparatory stage of discussion.

It is evident that a temporal relationship of antecedent and consequent will hold not so much between things as between states of things. Nor is it a simple relation between one state and another; it is rather a relation between a set of conditions and the outcome which they determine. In ordinary thinking we sometimes single out the last requisite condition to be supplied as being *the* cause of a change, but this is obviously not the attribution to it of any special causal efficacy; one of the other requisite conditions might equally have happened to be the last verified. More significantly, when a rational will is involved, we often speak of this as being *the* cause, for a will is a cause in a fuller sense because the effect is foreseen and intended. Nevertheless, no demonstration is needed that a human will is far from being the complete cause of any event.

The notion of causation in the temporal sense is, then, the conception of a set of conditions at one moment as determining some new state of things at the next moment. Objection might be made to speaking of moments in the history of the universe. It might be said, and it has been said, that the moments which we distinguish in processes of change are arbitrary insertions of reason. But, if anything really is, it is for some length of time, however small, and, although instances of continuous change may well occur, even continuous change must begin from being and end with being. There are, consequently, moments in the history of the universe, marked out by things or states or activities beginning to be, and the moments which we are able to distinguish in processes of change are arbitrary only in the sense that they are a selection, dictated by the direction of our attention and interest, from the innumerable multitude of real moments. Although a more penetrating intellect than the human would be able to entertain a more subtle and complete analysis of temporal process, the stages which we distinguish are really stages, and the relations which we perceive between them are relations which belong to the sphere of fact.

The objections made by Hume and Kant to regarding

causality as a factual relation are similar in principle and have been treated with far too much respect. Hume objects that the causal relation cannot be seen to follow from its terms in the same way as, for example, resemblance or mathematical relations; any concrete thing may be conceived as coming to be and as existing without the necessity of conceiving some other thing to be its cause. Kant maintains that the only kind of proposition which is evident on its own merits is the strictly analytic, in which the predicate is part of the analysis of the subject; a causal proposition is not one of this kind but an *a priori* synthesis, which is an application of the innate categories of the intellect, claiming no validity for things as they are in themselves. The question is, therefore, whether we can perceive a necessary conjunction of terms which are concretely distinct. Hume says that we cannot, but merely develop expectations after repeated experience; Kant says that we are able to do so only because we have ourselves imported the relationship into the facts. But the answer is that we just do perceive such relationships, and perceive them to be as much a part of the brute facts as the terms which they relate. Neither Hume's dogma that anything which can be separately conceived can exist separately nor Kant's dogma that only analytic propositions carry their evidence in themselves, has any foundation in intellectual experience.[1]

We see often enough, without any need of having repeated experience or of invoking an extraneous maxim, how one state or activity of mind naturally leads to another. Hume's own explanation of how we mistakenly come to believe in the causal relation involves the validity of the very causality

[1] Having previously treated at some length the objectivity of causation in opposition to Hume, Kant and their successors in a book on *Causality and Implication*, I content myself with a summary account here.

which he is denying. For it seemed natural to Hume, and it is indeed natural, that the repeated experience of two types of fact together should set up an association of ideas, so that, when the thought of one occurs in a mind which has acquired this habit of association, the thought of the other is thereby caused to occur. This does not provide, as Hume thought, an adequate *explanation* of the meaning of causality, but any association of ideas is a satisfactory *instance* of the kind of causality which we immediately apprehend in the mental realm.

Once provided with the notion of causality, we can look for instances of it where this immediate insight is not available, and we can recognize in general that whatever begins to exist must have an origin in something already existent. We do not, it should be remarked, perceive that the state of the universe at one moment wholly determines its state at the next. The free choices of a rational will must be instances of agency but not of complete antecedent causation, and, if there is a non-temporal being, this being will exercise causal determination in yet another and non-temporal sense. Causality as a temporal relation does not, therefore, yield a principle of universal determination; we have simply to acknowledge that instances of such causality occur and are worth looking for in the pursuit of the rational interpretation of fact, but we cannot assert that the whole source of whatever begins to exist is to be found in its temporal antecedents. We can, however, see in general that the natures of things are tendencies which work themselves out in time and that the state of the universe at one moment at least partially determines the state of the universe at the next. This conception of temporal causation is a primary acknowledgment of reason, and there is nothing more to say about it except to elucidate it and to invite people to notice it.

4

Since Kant holds that the categorial relation of cause and effect is an importation of the mind and can be thought to subsist only between possible phenomena in space and time, he evidently cannot accept any argument for the existence of God based upon causality. Against the Kantian view of causality, however, we have already protested. He also objects against the causal argument that it is inefficacious except in conjunction with the ontological argument; to this we shall have to refer later. What is at present relevant is his attempt to show that, if the category of cause and effect is extended beyond the sphere of phenomena, it leads to contradictions; this is the line of thought which we find in the section on the antinomies in the *Critique of Pure Reason.*

While this issue is raised explicitly in the third and fourth antinomies, an important preliminary appears in the first. Here Kant maintains that it can be argued with equal plausibility that the world has existed for a finite time and that it had no beginning. The proof of the *thesis,* that the world has existed for a finite time, is said to rest upon the nature of an infinite series, which is such that it cannot be completely traversed or exhausted in a succession of steps. But at any given moment the time-series is completed by that moment; hence it is a finite series. The proof of the *antithesis,* that the world had no beginning, depends upon the Kantian assumption that time is immediately given as an infinite whole within which events occur. Then, if the world had existed only for a finite time, history would be bounded by empty time. But there is no character in empty time by which anything could be brought to exist at this moment rather than that, or indeed could be brought to exist at all. Consequently, since things exist, things have always existed.

We can at once dispose of this alleged proof of the antithesis. St. Augustine had, in fact, already refuted it in anticipation. *Non est mundus factus in tempore sed cum tempore.*[1] Empty time is only a fiction, and, until changeable things exist, there is no real time. Hence, if the world had a beginning, time also had a beginning. The world might have existed longer than it has existed, but to this truth corresponds a mere possibility and not a reality prior to the actual existence of the world. The beginning of the world must then be conceived to depend not upon something prior to it in time but upon something which is timeless. Therefore Kant's dialectical proof that the world must be eternal is not very impressive, even as dialectics.

The thesis is more interesting. Can it be demonstrated that the world had a beginning? This question was debated in the Middle Ages with greater subtlety than Kant brought to the task. The Averroists of the thirteenth century, in this respect faithful disciples of Aristotle, maintained that, at any rate as far as a philosopher could see, the world was eternal. The Arabic philosophers had generally held the same view, although the Jewish thinker Maimonides had suggested that neither the reasons for it nor the reasons against it amounted to a demonstration. St. Albert the Great thought that, if the creation of matter were admitted, it could be proved that the world had a beginning. St. Bonaventure maintained that both creation and the existence of the world for no more than a finite time were susceptible of demonstration on purely philosophical grounds. In the opinion of St. Thomas Aquinas, while the fact of creation could be proved, it could not be shown philosophically that

[1] St. Augustine: *De Civitate Dei*, XI. 6.

the world had a beginning. Durandus, introducing a new distinction, held that an unchanging created thing might have existed eternally, but that a series of changes must be finite. Among the later scholastics Suarez followed Durandus, but Vazquez modified this view by asserting that a cyclical series might have existed eternally, so that the heavenly bodies and their motions, as they were conceived to be according to Aristotelian physics and Ptolemaic astronomy, might have had no beginning.[1]

The mediaeval thinkers usually discussed this question in connection with the notion of creation, after they had already demonstrated the existence of God. We are now raising the issue at an earlier stage of our inquiry. Is it compatible with the nature of a temporal thing that it should have had no beginning? Time implies changeability; an absolutely unchangeable thing has not an existence drawn out in time. Nevertheless time does not imply actual change; although it is hard to think of a temporal thing as completely unchanging, the combination of concepts involves no contradiction. With such a thing, if it existed, there would be no difficulty about an infinite series. Hence we may agree with Durandus that such a thing is thinkable and might have existed for an infinite time.

We may also admit the point made by Vazquez that a purely cyclical type of change is reducible to unchangingness. If a series of motions or other changes comes round at a definite period to the same state again, the system is on a wider view an unchanging one. Such a system might also, as far as we can judge from its mere notion, have had no beginning. This brings to mind that the hypothesis of a cyclical history of the universe has in fact, as with the Stoics,

[1] A useful collection of texts about this disputed question may be found in M. Gierens: *Controversia de Aeternitate Mundi* (Rome, 1933).

been a favourite device for overcoming the imaginative difficulty of supposing unending time.

But what should we say about a series of changes which is not cyclical or eventually repetitive? The argument put forward dialectically by Kant and seriously by Bonaventure and others is that such a series must be finite, for at any given moment it is completed and at the next it is added to, whereas an infinite series has no termination and cannot be augmented. Really, however, this kind of argument is not very convincing. An infinite series presents an imaginative rather than a strictly intellectual difficulty. We can certainly conceive, although we cannot imagine, an indefinite series stretching out into the future. An indefinite series reaching back into the past is a greater stumbling-block for the imagination, for we are inclined vaguely to suppose that, unless we can arrive at some first point from which to reverse the process and return to the present, time itself could never have arrived at the present moment. But we must not impose upon fact the limitations of our power of counting. If we cannot, in Kantian phrase, produce a successive synthesis of an infinite series, it by no means follows that such a series cannot exist. There seems to be no greater difficulty of a genuinely intellectual kind in the notion of an infinite series in the past than there is in the notion of an infinite series in the future.

Nor does there appear to be any overwhelming difficulty in an infinite time-series being added to from moment to moment. Modern developments in the mathematics of infinite numbers have accustomed us to the thought of one infinite number being greater than another. A time-series which is unbounded in the past but bounded by an ever-growing present offers no apparent absurdity. Hence, in the end, we must agree with St. Thomas that no peremptory reason can be provided by philosophy for the assertion that the world and its processes of change have existed for a finite time.

Nevertheless, if it were to be held that the world had existed for an infinite time, we should have to give up the common theory of progressive evolution as a clue to its history. A progressive evolution must have a beginning in relation to which later events can be evaluated. Hence, in the hypothesis of a world without a beginning, while a part of its history might be construed in terms of progressive evolution, this would be a contingent fact about that part of history and not a general principle of historical interpretation. So far, then, from evolutionary doctrine excluding a creator, it rather emphasizes the necessity of a creator by demanding the explanation of a beginning. The factual evidence for progressive evolution as a key to the history of the universe has no more than the force which belongs to a scientific hypothesis, but, whatever force it possesses, it is a motive towards the acceptance of a divine purpose unfolding itself in the world.

On the whole, current speculations in physics about the age of the universe are favourable to the view that the material world had an origin at some enormous but still finite distance of time. This and its bearing on theism have been emphasized by Sir Edmund Whittaker.[1] We shall not, however, exploit this line of thought, because scientific hypotheses have not sufficient certainty to be the foundation of a metaphysical argument. We shall follow the absolutely stringent method of philosophy and indulge in no pre-supposition about whether the world had a beginning or not.

[1] Cf. Sir Edmund Whittaker: *The Beginning and End of the World* and *Space and Spirit*.

5

Whether the world has existed for a finite or for an infinite time, some necessary being must be admitted. If anything exists at all, there must be some necessary being, for what is contingent could not exist except in dependence upon what is necessary. Moreover, we must recognize that whatever begins to be, or ceases to be, is contingent and exists as the effect of something else. Hence the process of history is a field of contingency, and we rightly seek to explain what comes to be by what has preceded it. If the world had an absolute beginning, we must obviously look for some cause outside it. In the supposition that the world has existed for an infinite time, we must still look to something which neither begins nor ceases to be, for an explanation of those things or states which begin to be and cease to be. A consideration of time and change has so far led us to the conclusion that only what neither begins nor ends can possess necessary existence.

This is evident enough, but we cannot dispense ourselves from examining what Kant has to say. At this important stage of the argument, moreover, it seems incumbent upon us not only to report Kant's objections and to attack them with the aid of principles different from his, but to try to enter into his mind and to assess the real foundation of his denials. For Kant's predilection for architectonic often led him to yield the foreground to formal considerations which had comparatively little to do with why he really thought as he did, and his unstated premises are frequently more momentous than those which he states. When we begin to explore his background, we find that he is not merely a perverse academic thinker in an ivory tower; he typifies and gives theoretical expression to a state of mind which he shares with many in modern times who are not philosophers at all.

Nothing is more basic to an understanding of Kant than to appreciate the impression produced on his mind by the rapid expansion of a physical science which was mechanistic and mathematical. There seemed to lie the ideal of theoretical knowledge, yet Kant, far more than his eighteenth-century contemporaries, grasped the truth that this sort of knowledge, while it is a genuine apprehension of structure and relationships, can never reveal precisely what the things are with which it is concerned. The physicists of our own day are in a state of embarrassment because this is now generally understood, but Kant in his remote and oracular way had effectively said it long ago.

Hence, in his theory of knowledge, the very objects which we envisage and notions which we employ in ordinary thinking become hypotheses which we construct, rather than facts or aspects of fact of which we become aware. Ordinary thinking is only a less systematic kind of scientific thinking, and, given Kant's restricted view of scientific thinking, his view of the nature of ordinary thinking becomes more intelligible. At any rate, as far as our present subject is concerned, it was evidently firmly impressed upon his mind that the only notion of causality which could find a place in mechanistic science was that of a temporal relation of determining antecedent and determined consequent. It is, therefore, this notion of causality which he erects into an essential category of the intellect, which alone belongs to the sphere of theoretical knowledge, but which is applicable only to phenomena and not to things in themselves. Although he was perfectly well aware of other possible types of causality, and these have an indispensable function in the activity of the practical reason, they do not for him come within the scope of exact theoretical knowledge.

Against this background the argument of the third and fourth antinomies can be appreciated. On the assumption that the categorical relation of cause and effect can alone be a source of theoretical knowledge, Kant tries to show what contradictions result from supposing that theoretical knowledge is of things in themselves and not merely of phenomena. If he is aiming at demonstrating the inadequacy of theoretical thinking in fact, he is equally looking forward to exhibiting a knowledge of fact which is not purely theoretical and scientific. On the one side he argues, much as we have argued, that, if anything exists, the totality of the conditions of its existence must be presupposed. Hence not everything can be conditioned; if the conditioned exists, the unconditioned must exist also as its ultimate antecedent. The causality of the unconditioned cannot itself be a conditioned causality; it must be a free and spontaneous agency which is not brought into exercise by anything other than itself.

So far so good, but on the other side Kant insists that the only admissible theoretical notion of causality is the temporal relationship of antecedent and consequent. If this is so, there cannot be an antecedent which is not also a consequent; there cannot be an agency which comes into play spontaneously without any extrinsic determination. An absolutely first temporal antecedent is unthinkable because we at once have to ask in virtue of the principle of causality what determines it at any definite time to produce a consequent. Thus, while we are trying to think of it as absolutely first, it necessarily ceases to be absolutely first and demands a more ultimate cause to bring it into action. Kant concludes that there is no other way out of this conflict but to admit that

theoretical knowledge is not of things as they are in themselves; it is of phenomena and always retains the unfinished
character which besets our acquaintance with phenomena.
If we are to make use of notions such as necessary existence
and spontaneous agency, it can only be in virtue of some
other function of mind than the exact and scientific.

The modern mind has now to some extent caught up with
Kant, and it is commonly held that we have an immense
body of exact knowledge about nothing in particular, while
in relation to absolute fact we have to content ourselves with
ignorance or with the deliverances of aspiration. What are
we going to reply to this attitude of mind, whether as
represented by the average contemporary or as prophetically
articulated by Kant? Our reply is that this restriction of the
sphere of exact knowledge is wholly mistaken; it is a contingent
historical result of the great expansion of the physical sciences
in modern times. It is not the function of the sciences to
dictate to philosophy but of philosophy to interpret and to
govern the particular sciences. If the notions employed by
philosophy do not find a place in one or other of the sciences,
this implies not the uncertainty of philosophy but the
incompleteness of the sciences.

In the matter of causality it is entirely gratuitous to
suppose that, because the temporal relationship of antecedent and consequent is the appropriate conceptual
instrument in a mechanistic science, this is the only exact
and scientific notion of cause and effect. If, with a more
adequate general theory of knowledge than Kant possessed,
we recognize that ordinary thinking is at once in contact
with real fact and not merely with appearance, we must
recognize also that we cannot be content with the temporal
notion of causation. Useful as it is for the interpretation of
historical change, the quest of intelligibility compels us by

the very force of reason to transcend it. Kant's antitheses in the third and fourth antinomies are the expression of a specific exercise of reason which is content with its own limitations. When we reject Kant's dichotomy and acknowledge that reason is one, we must acknowledge also that necessary being exists and that its relationship to contingent being is other than the temporal relationship of antecedent to consequent. If we can see, as we should see, that this is just as much an acknowledgment of exact and scientific thinking as is the employment of the temporal notion of causality in the subordinate sciences, we shall not be agitated by Kant's scruples.

History, then, is contingent. Whatever begins to be or ceases to be, owes its existence to something other than itself. If anything exists, necessary being exists. Necessary being neither begins to be nor ceases to be. Beneath or beyond the flux of historical process we must find something permanent. Here is our next question. Is necessary being beneath or beyond history? Is it the substratum of change or an agent exempt from change? Materialists assert that necessary being is the substratum of change. Can this contention be reasonably upheld?

CHAPTER III

THE INADEQUACY OF MATERIALISM

I

IN WESTERN philosophy those who have claimed to find necessary being within the world of experience have generally been materialists. This is not inevitable. It might be supposed that minds formed an independent group of eternal entities. The transmigration of souls would, of course, naturally enter into such a theory, as it often does in Eastern thought. This is a logically gratuitous doctrine, for there is no positive evidence in its favour; all the evidence points to our minds having originated and developed along with our bodies. The rational tradition of Western thought has, therefore, been unwilling to adopt it. Hence in concentrating our attention upon materialism, we shall be facing a more substantial adversary, but what we shall have to say in opposition will be applicable to any theory which holds that necessary being is to be found within the world of experience.

Materialism makes its appearance as a primitive and unsophisticated attempt to interpret the world rationally. The first Greek philosophers, Thales and the other Ionians, seem to have taken as their main question, what the world is made of. Their answers, whether in terms of water or of air or of whatever else, are implicitly materialistic; it is better to add the qualification of implicitness, for we can hardly tell what logical status they attributed to their hypotheses or whether they thought that these offered a complete solution of the constitution of the world. At any rate they exemplify the truth that an inquiry into the nature of the visible and tangible is one of the first and most obvious tasks which offer themselves to the human mind when it begins to think scientifically.

Greek thought, however, did not linger in materialism. Even if the forces of love and hate described by Empedocles as governing the activity of the elements be merely anthropomorphic expressions for something like attraction and repulsion, the traces of the dominant activity of mind in the universe became increasingly apparent. The naïve wonder of the early Pythagoreans at the exact numerical relations which are exemplified in the interchanges of material things led the way to the recognition by Socrates and Plato of the supremacy of the intelligible over the merely sensible. It is scarcely necessary to recall the passage in which Plato represents Socrates as speaking of the sense of liberation with which he came across the opinion of Anaxagoras that mind was the ultimate cause and source of order, and at the same time the disappointment which he felt upon finding how little use Anaxagoras made of this doctrine in detail.[1] With Socrates and Plato, however, the main stream of Greek philosophy took a decisive turn away from the shallows of materialism.

Nevertheless, at much the same time as Socrates, Democritus was expanding the atomic theory of Leucippus and giving to materialism a form in which it has constantly recurred. In modern times also it has been found that the most convenient conceptual instrument for interpreting the material world is the hypothesis of minute particles whose association and dissociation provoke the changes which are

[1] Plato: *Phaedo*, 97–9.

observable by the senses. Even if, at the present moment, the notion of ultimate particles is questioned by physicists, this may well be the result only of special and temporary embarrassments in the development of physical science, for no equally intelligible alternative appears to be available. While an atomic theory thus seems to have an assured place in the sphere of being to which the principles of mechanistic science are applicable, it in no way follows that a complete philosophy of the universe can rest upon it; the dominant voice of Greek thought in its maturity proclaims that much more is required.

Among the later Greeks, the Epicureans, fatigued and despairing of wider speculation, recurred to the materialism of Democritus, but, on the whole, apart from the solitary mediaeval figure of David of Dinant, " who crassly supposed that God was first matter ",[1] materialism makes no impressive reappearance until modern times. Here the impulse has come not so much from the internal development of philosophy itself as from the immense expansion of the physical sciences. Two illegitimate inferences have, with more or less explicitness, been drawn from the growth of science. The first step is to suppose that the material world offers the only field of exact knowledge; the second is to conclude that nothing exists except matter, or at least that anything else possesses a transient existence dependent upon matter.

In the seventeenth century, of course, Hobbes managed somewhat obscurely to combine theism with materialism, but it was naturally at the cost of being unable to assert anything positive about God. The real source of modern materialism is surely to be found in the French thinkers of the eighteenth century, the Encyclopaedists and those

[1] St. Thomas Aquinas: *Summa Theologica*, I qu. 3 art. viii c.

akin to them. La Mettrie, Holbach and Diderot in his later period present us with the now familiar picture of an eternal matter bearing in itself the germs of all the developments of recorded and unrecorded history and gradually evolving into life and mind as we know them. Thinking is wholly a product of the brain, and nothing beyond the world is required in order to explain what the world is and becomes. Marx and Engels had little to add, except the conceptual apparatus of Hegelian dialectic, in order to construct what has been the most practically effective system of thought in recent times. The great literary success of the French Encyclopaedists explains also why many today who are not.Marxists, and who would not even describe themselves positively as materialists, have as a part of the permanent background of their minds a picture of the world and its history which is essentially materialistic.

2

The influence of materialism, whether acknowledged or not, upon the contemporary mind is so pervasive that it deserves to be described in some detail. What we shall have to say is applicable in considerable measure to philosophers as well as to the man in the street. The modern man is aware, in a general way at least, of the great forward strides which the physical sciences have taken since the seventeenth century. The applications of science are all around him in his house and in his means of travel when he leaves it. When a war breaks out, the might of applied science becomes even more clearly, although painfully, evident to him.

It is small wonder, therefore, that he unreflectively tends to assume that the physical sciences represent the ideal of exact knowledge. The physicist, the chemist, the biologist are for him just simply the scientists, those who know. If he studied logic, he would understand that, while he was not overrating the increase in scientific knowledge, he was certainly overrating the degree of precision and certainty which can be attributed to the results of the physical sciences, but even some philosophers would send him away with the notion that philosophy can do little more than comment upon scientific method and construct a synthesis of the sciences. At any rate his working picture of the world is based upon current scientific theory in so far as this is made accessible to him, whether through popular outlines of history and outlines of science or through any more intimate acquaintance that he is able to attain.

Astronomy has shown him the enormous size of the physical universe, in which he is a speck upon a planet revolving round one of a myriad suns, and, like Pascal, he is appalled by his material insignificance. But he does not follow Pascal in making the complementary reflection that with his mind he is able to grasp the immensity of space and to comprehend something of what it contains. That would be an intellectual reflection, and it occurs to him less easily than the previous imaginative impression. He continues to see himself as the tiny and transitory product of a vast cosmic evolution of matter.

Periods before the development of modern science seem to him primitive and barbarous, and their ideas unworthy of attention. Mediaeval thought has been neglected throughout modern times, but a classical education used to provide a corrective for this superficial reading of human history. With the decay of classical studies we are now confronted with a more widespread ignorance of the elements of civilization which are not, in the contemporary sense, scientific.

The ordinary man may not know a great deal of the sciences in detail, but they are concerned with what is visible and tangible, and the outline of their methods can be described in visible and tangible terms. Hence imagination can assist understanding in coping with them, and the ordinary man feels at home with them. The intellectual *instinct* which led even primitive man to know himself for something more than matter has been weakened, and the *explicit process* of philosophical thinking which would lead to the same conclusion appears too difficult. Lacking the imaginative vividness which belongs to the sciences of the material world, it seems remote and ineffectual.

Where the higher intellectual instinct is entirely suppressed, pure materialism is adopted. It has not, however, always or even usually disappeared completely; it survives as a source of feeling and aspiration. In either case, nevertheless, the result is much the same as far as the conception of knowledge is concerned. Knowledge, for the modern man, means the physical sciences; what is outside their scope is regarded as strictly unknowable, whether it be admitted as a field of vague speculation or not.

In opposition to this climate of opinion the philosopher who maintains the autonomy and supremacy of philosophy has to assert the possibility, the exactness and the certainty of genuine philosophical thinking. If the ordinary man no longer finds intellectual instinct enough, he must be shown how to think philosophically, at least in an elementary way. The confidence in philosophy of philosophers themselves must be restored. At any rate what we have to do here is not to propose any new scientific hypotheses or any new interpretation of the results of the sciences; acknowledging the validity of the sciences in their own sphere, we have to ask profounder questions than the sciences can ask or answer, and we have to treat these questions in a properly philosophical way. We have to inquire whether materialism can be philosophically upheld as a final explanation of the universe.

3

If necessary being can be found in the ultimate particles of matter, it follows that the material world has always existed. Hence it would naturally be assumed that the material world has passed through an infinite series of changes, and that it had no first state upon which its history might be conceived as depending in causal sequence. If it were, somewhat fantastically, supposed that it persisted without change for an infinite time and that afterwards its history began at a finite distance of time from the present, the existence of some cause outside the material world to initiate the series of changes would be evident.

ˎ The hypothesis to be seriously considered is, therefore, that matter is necessary and everlasting and that the past history of the material world is an infinite series of events. In that case, in accordance with the temporal principle of causality, each momentary state of the universe is dependent upon the state which preceded it. But, if there is an infinite series of events stretching back into the past, every member of this series is preceded by another member. Every member of the series is, consequently, causally dependent. But a series of which all the members are effects as well as causes is not self-explanatory. A collection or series of effects demands a cause just as much as a single effect. Therefore, in the hypothesis that there has been an infinite series of events in the past, this series must be conceived as causally dependent in another and non-temporal sense upon something outside the series.

Upon what could history then be supposed to depend? It might be suggested that history represents the working out of the potentialities of the ultimate particles of matter themselves. In their successive forms of association and dissociation they would initiate the qualities and activities which are manifested in the stream of events. The non-temporal cause of the infinite temporal series would then be constituted by the persistent ultimate particles of matter.

But, if matter is necessary, and if any system of relationships between the particles of matter follows necessarily from the nature of matter, this structure or configuration of the material world must itself be necessary and everlasting. If, on the other hand, the configuration of the material world changes, it cannot follow simply from the nature of matter but demands a cause outside the material world. The choice is, consequently, between a static world and a world in which there is change but in which this change demands an external source. We know, however, that the world is not static but constantly changing. Hence there is outside it a cause of change which is itself unchanging.

The appearance of reasonableness in the hypothesis which we are criticizing is due to the analogy of life. A living thing has its characteristic mode of change and development which is a part of its nature. The materialistic doctrine considers material particles on the analogy of living things as possessing an inexhaustible tendency to new combinations and activities. The analogy fails because the living things of experience have a beginning of existence. With something whose substantial existence is thus temporally limited, there is no difficulty in conceiving its history as a gradual unfolding of innate potentialities; it is a thing subject to time in its very nature. On the materialistic hypothesis, however, the case is different. The existence of the ultimate material particles has neither beginning nor end; although they are thought of as subject to extrinsic change in their relationships, they are in their essential nature timeless. But a timeless nature cannot be an internal principle of temporal change; what is timeless is timelessly all that it must be. If it belongs to its nature to be in this or that relation to something else, it exists in such a relationship eternally and unalterably. If, then, we want to conceive of a timeless nature as subject to change of relationship, we must admit that the source of such change is something different and unchanging.

It follows, therefore, that materialism is inadequate as a final explanation of the universe. We have not yet shown that matter is not necessarily existent; a more direct examination of the demands of necessary existence is first required. But we have shown that material particles cannot be the sole necessary existents; if they existed necessarily, the changes in the configuration of the material world would have to come from another source. Generalizing our line of thought, we have to say that things subject to change, even if they be supposed to persist in their essential nature, cannot be the sole necessary existents. Neither minds such as our own nor material particles nor both can be the sole necessary existents. There must exist a necessary being which is in no way subject to change, a being which is eternal or completely timeless.

Casting our minds back, we observe in this reasoning a development of the concept of cause. It is in no sense an arbitrary or gratuitous development; it is enforced upon us by the nature of reality. In our thinking about the things of experience we employ the notion of causality as the relation between determining temporal antecedents and determined consequent. Moreover, at any moment of time, we think of the total situation as the result of the interaction of the things concerned in it; we think of things as possessing powers both in themselves to manifest qualities and activities and to affect and be affected by other things. Here we find the other current causal notion of agency and correlative passivity. In following out these principles of explanation we are faced with an alternative. Either the temporal causal series and the existence of temporal agencies had a beginning or they had not. If they had no beginning, an infinite series of causes all of which are effects is not self-sufficing; nor could the agency of things which have neither beginning nor end of existence, and whose essential being is timeless, serve as an explanation of the changes of state and relationship which they themselves undergo. In either case, therefore, we have in the end to look for a cause of a different kind. There must be something which is completely timeless and unchanging in itself but which, at the stage of the argument which we have at present reached, we recognize to be the source either of the whole being of temporal things or at least of contingent relations and changes in time. The causality of such a being is that not of a first temporal antecedent, but of a non-temporal agency, with an equal originative relation to the whole of history past, present and future.

CHAPTER IV

THE CAUSAL ARGUMENT

I

IN THE previous two chapters we have developed the causal or cosmological argument in a mainly indirect fashion, by showing the inadequacy of the opinions which contradict it. We cannot suppose the process of history as a whole to be self-explanatory, if it consists of things and events of which none are themselves self-explanatory. Without needing to specify what kinds of dependence in being are instantiated in the real world, we can say that there must be something which is independently real. If everything were supposed to be dependent upon something else, we should be involved in a vicious circle, for the whole process would have to hang upon literally nothing. Hence there must be some necessary being. We went on to show that there must be at least some necessary being which is exempt from change. If, on the materialistic hypothesis, all necessary beings were subject to change, there would be nothing to explain how actual changes come to be. Therefore we must admit at least one necessary being which is a source of change but is not itself subject to change; that is, we must admit at least one necessary being different from the objects of experience or what may be supposed to be their fundamental elements.

This inference may be presumed, in its general outline, to be as old as human reflection, and it amounts to what has been called the causal or cosmological argument for the

existence of God. When we look for its explicit expression
in exact terms in the history of our own civilization, we find
it first of all among the Greeks in the argument for a first
mover or cause of change. Plato, by the argument which
he presents in the tenth book of the *Laws*, is the father of our
explicit natural theology. Already in the *Phaedrus* he had
argued more briefly and in general that soul, as being an
original source of movement or change, must be immortal,
having neither a beginning nor an end of its existence.[1] This
line of thought, as A. E. Taylor has pointed out, was
associated by Aristotle with the reasoning of Alcmaeon of
Croton that soul must be immortal because it is akin to the
immortal things, like sun, moon and stars, which are in
perpetual motion.[2] In the same passage, moreover, Aristotle
refers back to the opinion of Heraclitus that soul is at the
origin of things because it is most completely in a condition
of flux; here, of course, we must remember that Heraclitus
regards fire as being of the essence of soul or life.

The piquant conclusion suggests itself, therefore, that
Plato owes some of his theory of soul to that philosophy of
flux which in other connections he condemns rather severely.
This is not excessively astonishing. Since soul is so unlike
the Forms, it has to be examined on different principles,
and hints about it can be derived from thinkers whose blind-
ness to the unchanging Forms has elsewhere to be exposed
without mercy. But Platonism is a philosophy of soul as
well as of the Forms; there is no understanding of Plato
without giving equal weight to what he says about soul. Nor
is his view of the soul as pre-existent to its bodily life as well
as surviving it so unreasonable in the absence of a notion of

---

[1] Plato: *Phaedrus* 245–6.
[2] Aristotle: *De Anima*, I, ii. 405a–b. Cf. A. E. Taylor: *Plato, the Man
and his Work*, 4th ed., 1937, p. 306n.

creation. Plato, like the other Greeks, did not deny creation; they could not affirm or deny it because none of them had reached so far as to conceive its possibility. If, however, the possibility of creation is not taken into account, how could souls have arisen? They are different in kind from the energies of purely corporeal things and could not be a product of them. Hence it is natural to suppose that they have always existed.

In the *Laws* Plato makes use of his conception of soul in explaining the universe as a whole. It is likely that he is giving a genuine biographical detail when he represents Socrates in the *Phaedo* as complaining that, while Anaxagoras had represented mind as being the cause of order in the world, that philosopher made little particular use of his general principle.[1] The argument of the *Laws* endeavours to be at least a little more specific.[2] Plato begins with an elaborate classification of eight kinds of motion, a classification which turns out in the end to have no particular bearing upon his argument. This is a favourite device of Plato for slowing up the tempo of his dialogues and preparing for something of major importance, but a captious reader might complain that he uses it too freely. At any rate he arrives at his real point when he distinguishes two final varieties of motion, that which moves itself and that which is moved by another. But motion which is produced by another thing cannot be primary, for there must always be a prior thing to produce it. If there had ever been a state of absolute rest, it could never have produced itself; if not, a regress, however long, would never bring us to a genuine source of motion among things moved in this way. Hence the only genuinely originative motion must be self-moving. But to be self-

---

[1] Plato: *Phaedo*, 97–8.
[2] Plato: *Laws*, X, 891E–896C.

moving is characteristic of life or soul in opposition to mere body. Therefore soul is proved to be the ultimate source of change in the universe.

There is no assertion here of one supreme soul which is the single ultimate source of motion or change; indeed Plato expressly speaks of a number of such souls which animate or propel the heavenly bodies and which, as enjoying greater power and stability than human souls, must be accounted as gods. Moreover he attributes an independent activity to bad soul or souls, thereby explaining the evil in the universe. Nevertheless, he insists that the good souls which are the gods will not have less thought or care for others than the best men have. Consequently there is a divine providence for the universe, although it does not completely overcome the disturbing activities of bad soul. In this way Plato justifies the gods and their worship in the ideal state whose constitution he is discussing in the whole dialogue.

In the *Timaeus*, Plato offers a cosmogony or description of how the ordered universe may have come into existence. Here he speaks of a single supreme soul, the Demiurge or world-craftsman, who is the source of other souls as well as of the structure of the universe. Much of the dialogue must be judged to be mythical in the Platonic sense; that is, it is a description of what might reasonably be supposed in the absence of any certain knowledge of what actually was. The suggestion of a beginning of the cosmos can scarcely have been intended seriously by Plato. He had no conception of creation; the activity of the Demiurge is exercised upon a pre-existent matter or space understood as the potential recipient of participation in the Forms. Hence, if the cosmos had a beginning, there would have been a primeval chaos existing from infinite time; this can hardly have been meant literally. How literally, then, did Plato mean us to take the notion of the Demiurge? It has often been suggested that, in accordance with the general character of the dialogue, the Demiurge must also be interpreted as a symbolic figure. Yet Plato describes his ungrudging goodness in forming the universe with a piety which is difficult to reconcile with conscious symbolism. Therefore it is perhaps not too much to say that, although Plato offers no explicit argument for monotheism and does not hesitate to acknowledge many gods in the Greek sense of powerful immortal beings, he is nevertheless an instinctive monotheist. The quest of unity which led him to see the ideal world as governed by the Form of the Good must have led him also to think of the world of souls as subordinate to the supreme soul or Demiurge who is God in the full sense. At any rate Plato proposes an explicit argument that mind or soul is prior to body and is the ultimate source of motion or change and of the order of the universe.

2

'While Plato argues to self-moved movers, Aristotle ends with unmoved movers. That the contradiction is no more than apparent was pointed out by St. Thomas Aquinas with his usual large-mindedness. Plato, says St. Thomas, understood by motion any kind of activity, so that thinking and acting would be kinds of motion, but Aristotle took motion more strictly as a transition from potentiality to actuality. Hence there is no real difference in arriving finally at what Plato calls a self-moved mover and Aristotle an unmoved mover.[1]

Aristotle's demonstration is to be found in the seventh and eighth books of the *Physics*, and it is resumed and in some respects developed in *Metaphysics* λ. It depends upon the principle that everything that is moved is moved

[1] St. Thomas Aquinas: *Summa contra Gentiles*, I, 13.

by something which can in some way be distinguished from it.[1] A perusal of Aristotle's elaborate process of reasoning will show that this cannot be simply identified with a metaphysical principle of causality; it is a specific application whose terms require to be appropriately elucidated.

Aristotle distinguishes the living, which is in a sense self-moving, from what always requires to be moved by a thing other than itself. He also distinguishes motion in accordance with nature from motion by violence or contrary to nature. It will be remembered that his physics embrace the notions of the absolutely light and the absolutely heavy, so that air and fire naturally tend upwards and water and earth naturally tend downwards, each to its natural place. His argument will not be understood unless these outmoded notions are taken into account along with the enduring parts of his philosophy.

When things are moved in a manner contrary to their natures, there can be no doubt, he says, that they are moved by something other than themselves. In the case of living things, also, it is not too difficult to distinguish the part which moves from the part which is moved; in the last resort the source of vital movement is the soul or form of the organism. But Aristotle frankly recognizes the difficulty of assigning a cause of movement when an inorganic object moves in accordance with its nature, as when a stone falls or flames leap up. He is content in the end to regard as the cause of its movement that which originally made it a thing of such a nature, together with whatever removed the obstacle to its natural movement. Hence there is in every case some distinction of mover and moved.

It follows, on pain of an infinite regress, that there must be an unmoved mover at the origin of each series of communicated motions. Any soul or vital principle answers to

[1] Aristotle: *Physics*, VIII, 4.

Aristotle's general conception of unmoved mover, but souls in the sublunary world are subject to temporal generation; they will not explain the eternity of movement. For movement, according to Aristotle, must be eternal.[1] If it were not, how could it possibly have begun? For Aristotle, eternal means without beginning or end but not without before or after. He has neither the notion of simultaneous eternity nor that of creation. The material world has, then, always existed. If it were ever at absolute rest, it could not set itself in motion, nor does there appear to be any reason why a soul or souls should set it in motion at this moment rather than at that. Moreover, since time is the measure of motion, there must be an eternal motion with which the backward infinity of time corresponds. Therefore motion is eternal.

But an eternal motion must be circular.[2] If it turned at an angle, it would no longer be one movement. There does not seem to be any peremptory reason why it should not be any sort of wavy line that returns to its beginning, but Aristotle was saved from further embarrassment by thinking that he actually observed the eternal circular motions which governed the universe. For these were the motions of the heavenly spheres upon which were supposed to be carried round sun, moon, planets and stars. These celestial movements seemed to be plainly unchanging and eternal. There must, consequently, be an eternal unmoved mover, a soul or intelligence, animating or governing each of the heavenly spheres. These are the gods, and, according to the number of spheres required by the astronomical science of the period, there are probably either forty-seven or fifty-five gods. But Aristotle confesses that certainty about the number of the gods is impossible.[3]

[1] Aristotle: *Physics*, VIII, 1.   [2] Aristotle: *Physics*, VIII, 9.
[3] Aristotle: *Metaphysics*, λ 8.

The intelligence which governs the outermost sphere, that of the fixed stars, is, however, the supreme god, for the movements of the other spheres are dependent on the movement of this. This being must be conceived as the perfection of pure intelligence, thought eternally thinking itself in complete independence and unawareness of anything other than itself.[1] It moves the rest by the love or desire of itself.[2] This statement may not be as lyrical as it sounds; it may indicate merely that the first unmoved mover is essentially a final cause in the way that any form is the final cause of the natural movement of that which it informs, for everything strives towards the fulfilment of its form or entelechy.

Such, in brief, is Aristotle's own argument for a first unmoved mover, and, if we appreciate its rather mixed character, we shall not reproach the mediaeval Aristotelians for a slavish imitation of their master when they adapt it as an argument for a very different kind of God. We shall much rather be inclined to wonder, until we have studied the matter, how it survived the necessary transmutation. Nevertheless, in spite of the strange mixture of metaphysical acumen and unwarranted hypothesis, Aristotle's reasoning is a powerful effort of human thought and arrives at an imposing notion of pure intelligence as the ruling force in the universe.

3

In the *Summa contra Gentiles*, St. Thomas Aquinas appears willing to accept the notion of God as exercising an immediate action on the first celestial sphere and reproduces a great deal of Aristotle's reasoning.[3] He does not, of course,

---

[1] Aristotle: *Metaphysics*, λ 9.   [2] Aristotle: *Metaphysics*, λ 7.
[3] St. Thomas Aquinas: *Summa contra Gentiles*, I, 13.

accept Aristotle's thesis of the eternity of matter and motion, but points out that, if the world had a beginning, it is all the easier to show that it has a divine cause. Hence he treats the argument as one to prove that, even if the world had no beginning, there must still be a God to explain its existence and processes. This remains his constant attitude; he does not regard philosophical reasoning as adequate to demonstrate that the world in fact had a beginning. Moreover he makes an express reserve against the supposition that God actually animates the first celestial sphere, and the ulterior development of his argument is, as is natural, towards a God who is the creator of the world and who knows and cares for everything in it.

When he came to write the *Summa Theologica*, St. Thomas used the first mover argument as the First Way to prove the existence of God.[1] In this version he sheds all the details of Aristotelian physics and offers only the essential metaphysical elements of the proof. We cannot infer that he no longer accepted the validity of his adaptation of the full Aristotelian argument, for he may, not without justice, have considered merely that its details were unduly difficult for his readers; we can, however, infer that he did not consider them as necessary. In this form the argument is simply that everything that is moved or changed is moved or changed by something else; but, where there is a series of relationships of actual dependence, an infinite regress is impossible, for all members of the series would be dependent but dependent on nothing; hence there must be an unmoved mover.

Put in this manner the First Way differs only little from the Second, which comes next both in the *Summa Theologica* and the *Summa contra Gentiles*. Here St. Thomas points

[1] St. Thomas Aquinas: *Summa Theologica*, I, qu. 2, art. iii.

to the fact of causality and, as in the First Way, observes that, where there is a series of relationships of actual dependence of effect on cause, an infinite regress would involve contradiction. Hence there is an uncaused cause.

The Third Way of the *Summa Theologica*, which has no counterpart in the earlier work, is another variation of the causal argument. It contains two difficulties of interpretation, which are probably due to the form of reasoning being derived from Avicenna and Maimonides; St. Thomas seems to have reproduced it with the terms in which it was familiar to his contemporaries and, consequently, to have made use of expressions which are uncharacteristic of his own thought. The fact from which the argument begins is the fact of contingency; we know that some things are contingent for the simple reason that they come to be and cease to be. But it cannot be supposed that everything is contingent or capable of being or not being. If so, there would have been a time at which nothing existed, and from nothing nothing could ever come to be. This is an assertion of Maimonides; his thought appears to be that, if everything were contingent, contingent things would have existed from infinite time. But in infinite time every possibility would be verified. Now, if everything were contingent, one possible state of affairs would be a situation in which nothing at all existed. Hence, if infinite time had already elapsed, this hypothesis would have already been verified.[1]

Therefore not everything can be contingent, but something must exist necessarily. But we may distinguish between what is necessary of itself and what is necessary but derives its necessity from something other than itself. This distinction probably acquires its meaning from Avicenna,

[1] Cf. E. Gilson: *Le Thomisme*, ed. 2 (1922), pp. 60-1.

according to whom the supreme intelligence or God is necessary of himself but there are other pure intelligences which emanate necessarily from God. St. Thomas would then be arguing hypothetically; if anyone thinks like Avicenna, then let him see what follows. For it is impossible that all necessary existents should derive their necessity from something else. This would be contradictory, since there would be nothing from which they could derive their necessity. Consequently there must be something which is necessary of itself.

The essential process of thought behind each of these three ways is exceedingly simple. If there is something changing, there is something unchanging; if there is something caused, there is something uncaused; if there is something contingent, there is something necessary. The hypothesis is in each case verified in experience, and the conclusion follows. The evident existence of dependent and conditioned being shows the necessary existence of being which is independent and unconditioned.

A further remark must, however, be made. By dropping the dubious physical trappings of Aristotle's argument and bringing out its central metaphysical content, St. Thomas is unable to arrive at so specific a conclusion as Aristotle. Nothing is more evident than that there must be something unchanging, uncaused and necessary, but it does not yet appear what sort of thing this must be. When, at the conclusion of each proof, St. Thomas identifies this with God, he is anticipating the development of this thought. It is in later chapters of the *Summa contra Gentiles* and later questions and articles of the *Summa Theologica* that he shows that necessary being must be infinite, unique, and an eternal mind. This development depends mainly on his metaphysics of being. Meanwhile, on the causal argument alone, we must be content with the modest but fundamental truth that some necessary being exists.

4

A stock objection, specifically against the First Way, is derived from Newton's law of inertia: Every body perseveres in its state of rest or of uniform motion in a straight line, except in so far as it is compelled to change that state by impressed forces. Hence it is suggested that it is mistaken to suppose that every motion demands a mover. Newton's law is, of course, a well-founded generalization from observed facts, but that is not to say that it needs no philosophical interpretation. Nor must this interpretation be of such a kind as to involve the evident absurdity that change takes place without a cause. The necessity of a cause for any change has a rational evidence which imposes itself on the mind at a stage which is logically prior to and independent of any departmental scientific generalization.

As a matter of fact, the general idea of Newton's law, together with a reasonable philosophical interpretation, had suggested itself more than three centuries before Newton. In the fourteenth century, John Buridanus had put forward a theory of impetus. He supposed that, when a body was set in motion, it acquired a quality of impetus or momentum which kept it in motion until this was counteracted by other forces. This entirely reasonable theory does justice both to the causal principle and to the law of inertia. Hence it has been adopted by many modern Thomists, including Garrigou-Lagrange,[1] who refers to St. Thomas himself for confirmation. For St. Thomas says that an instrument may be said to be moved by an agent as long as it retains the

[1] Cf. R. Garrigou-Lagrange: *Dieu*, ed. 4 (1923), p. 253.

power which this impresses upon it; thus an arrow is moved by the archer as long as the impulse remains which is bestowed upon it by the archer.[1]

Other Thomists, in the name of a rigid principle which has no foundation either in Aristotle or in St. Thomas, decline to admit this simple explanation. Thus G. H. Joyce, for example, demands that there should always be a cause of movement outside that which is moved.[2] He objects to an inherent quality of momentum that it would be indifferently of any velocity and direction, that it would constantly produce new effects, and that its efficiency would continue indefinitely unless counteracted. But in any particular case the momentum is of a determinate velocity and direction, and it is the common characteristic of active powers that they constantly produce new effects and produce them indefinitely.

These objections, therefore, need not detain us, but they will serve as an example of the unfortunate results of mistaking the boundary between philosophy and the physical sciences. When, in the name of philosophy, an extremely shaky piece of deductive inference is offered in opposition to a well-established scientific generalization, the scientist is inclined to retort by denying the independent validity of philosophy and dismissing it as a primitive and inadequate substitute for exact science. This is, indeed, how Sir Edmund Whittaker reacts, although, while welcoming Buridanus's theory of impetus as an anticipation of Newton,[3] he takes a much less kindly view of its utilization by the contemporary Thomist.[4] It should be realized that

---

[1] St. Thomas Aquinas: *De Potentia*, qu. 3, art. xi, ad. 5.
[2] Cf. G. H. Joyce: *Principles of Natural Theology*, ed. 2 (1924), pp. 96–105.
[3] Sir Edmund Whittaker: *Space and Spirit*, p. 48.
[4] *Op. cit.*, pp. 142–3.

philosophy and physical science have each their proper field. Philosophical principles, such as the causal principle, are independent of scientific observation and hypothesis, but, when the philosopher descends to the arena and tries to produce a kind of deductive and *a priori* physics, he lays himself open to not unmerited derision. His business, in respect of the proper realm of physics, is to accept scientific generalizations with the degree of assent which is appropriate to them and to tell the scientist more precisely what they mean when brought within a more general frame of reference.

From this point of view the philosopher certainly has something to say to the physicist who maintains that separate space and time have been abolished in favour of space-time, or that there is a genuine indeterminacy, contradicting the causal principle, in the time of dissolution of a radium atom.[1] He must insist that space and time remain precisely what they were and are to immediate awareness; all that a physicist can say is that it is impossible to measure them with complete exactness in isolation, but, if the physicist does say this, his conclusion is to be respected. Equally it must be insisted that no physical investigation can possibly reveal the absence of a cause; it could only reveal in some specific case that it was impossible to discover the agency at work. Even if this ignorance could never be overcome, the causal principle would retain precisely the same validity as before.

Another remark of Sir Edmund Whittaker about the theory of impetus deserves separate consideration. He says that, " if it is admitted that the mover may be no more than a mere accident of the ' moved ', the principle becomes inadequate to bear the weight of the argument for theism

[1] *Op. cit.*, pp. 110–12.

which is based on it."[1] Now, curiously enough, Aristotle's treatment of the movement of a body, when an obstacle is removed, towards its natural place offers, in terms of a different and admittedly mistaken physics, a sufficiently exact parallel. In such a case the present cause of movement must really be the absolute lightness or heaviness of the body itself. As we have already described, Aristotle's argument for a first unmoved mover takes this case into account. Nevertheless, as we have also pointed out, Aristotle's reasoning does not arrive at a conclusion which can be called theistic without assuming other dubious hypotheses. A Thomist must say that the first mover argument is not a complete argument for theism; it merely lays a foundation by presenting the very obvious truth that the occurrence of change presupposes an unchanging cause of change. That, in the end, there is only one unchanging cause of change, which is infinite being and eternal mind, depends upon a metaphysic of being which carries us far beyond the mere consideration of motion or change. If we are content with the genuine but modest conclusion which is entailed by the causal argument, we can see that specific physical theories, however true and important in their own sphere, make no difference to metaphysics.

5

We have already had occasion to mention the views of Hume and of Kant; at the end of this more historical chapter we can see them in their place in the movement of European thought. They are still with us; the objections made today against the causal argument are still those of Hume and of Kant. When, for example, we listen to

[1] *Op. cit.*, p. 143.

Bertrand Russell on causality, we are only listening to a reborn Hume.

We cannot dispose of Hume and Kant by offering simply a rectification of what they say about causality and the causal argument. Their philosophies repose upon entire misunderstandings of the nature of thinking, and we cannot expect to convince their followers by anything less than a vindication of the proper character of intellectual knowledge. What we say here relies for its full force upon a complete conception of intellect.

Hume is, in effect, the philosophical counterpart of the man who says that he believes only what he sees. After the sterile dialectic of the fourteenth and fifteenth centuries, it was necessary to re-examine the notions and principles which were the philosopher's stock-in-trade. The great achievement and still greater promise of seventeenth-century physical science showed that there was an immensely fruitful way of knowledge which stuck close to perceptual experience not only in the discovery of its concepts but also in the formulation and testing of its conclusions. It was not sufficiently realized that all this scientific development demanded for its interpretation and justification a logic and theory of knowledge which could not be otherwise than a deliverance of pure thinking. Hence it was natural to look for a renaissance of philosophy to a more painstaking scrutiny of experience.

This change in the direction of philosophical interest was far from being fruitless. The analysis and criticism of commonsense experience was an obligatory task which philosophers had not so far systematically faced. Unfortunately, however, as is usual in human affairs, the change was too radical. Philosophers became afraid to affirm anything which was not enforced upon them by their senses. Together with a great deal of useless verbiage, they threw overboard notions which are essential to any rational interpretation of the world.

That lack of even an ordinary degree of philosophical subtlety which is characteristic of Locke began the process of negation, and Hume owes his important place in the history of thought to having employed a considerable degree of philosophical subtlety in bringing the destructive process to its logical conclusion. Hume jettisons the entire baggage of intellectualism and views the result with cynical amusement. No philosophy is less credible than Hume's, but the example of his intellectual suicide continues to exercise a fatal attraction upon many contemporary minds.

His reduction of causality to a customary association of ideas owes whatever plausibility it possesses to an appeal to unsophisticated sense-experience. When we observe one billiard ball setting another in motion, we do not see anything passing from one to the other. This is not surprising, because, literally speaking, nothing does pass from one to the other. But Hume's point is that we observe nothing but first one ball in motion and then both; we do not externally observe any connection between the two motions but a temporal sequence. This is plainly true, and any attempt to derive our notion of causality from the behaviour of billiard balls is doomed to failure. The case, however, is altogether different when we attend to the sphere of mind and notice the relations between thoughts and other thoughts, between thoughts and feelings, and between thoughts, feelings and volitions. There we simply observe relationships which are the real counterpart of the logical relation of entailment, and we can see why, by analogy with them, we interpret the transactions of billiard balls in the same way. Hume is not only wrong but obviously wrong, and his mistake is due to a failure to attend to the relevant facts. The answer to him is given, not by a philosophy which despises experience, but by a philosophy which really does justice to the whole of experience.

The Kantian philosophy is commonly represented as a reaction to Hume, and this has its truth, but it must be supplemented by the acknowledgment that Kant is a wholly insufficient reaction to Hume. Kant's excuse may be that there was no more impressive contemporary representative of intellectualism than Christian Wolff. If this is a personal excuse, it is certainly not an objective justification. It remains true that Kant accepted the validity of Hume's denials in reference to a mere inspection of fact; he could recognize notions, like causality, only as a means of imposing order upon fact, and making it a possible object of human experience. If such notions are simply presented to us as themselves a matter of fact, there is no foundation for Kantian phenomenalism. But a more adequate scrutiny of experience shows that these notions are simple deliverances of experience. Consequently there is no foundation for Kantian phenomenalism.

Is this too cavalier a treatment of Kant? Many will certainly think so, but what else is there to say? It can only be repeated that the remedy for Kant, as for Hume, is not an elaborate refutation of his opinions in detail, but a recognition that his presuppositions were erroneous and that, consequently, he either attacked unreal problems or attacked real problems in the wrong way. People must therefore be invited to consider the issues afresh, and to perceive that the Kantian question does not arise. For Hume was wrong in supposing that the causal relation is not objectively presented in experience, and it follows that we do not have to ask how the mind imports it into experience.

Being is either dependent on other being or not. All being cannot be dependent on other being, for thus there would be no being upon which it could depend. Therefore there is some being which is independent of other being and necessary of itself. We have to ask what sort of being necessary being must be.

CHAPTER V

INFINITE BEING

I

THE first stage of the philosophical approach to God is to acknowledge that there must be some necessary being; we have next to see that necessary being can only be infinite being. The ontological argument, of course, proceeds in the reverse direction and asserts that the very concept of infinite being entails necessary existence. If this were so, our discussion could begin here; it would not have been required to make clear first that some necessary being exists. It is because we think that the ontological argument reverses the genuine order of thought that we began with a demonstration of necessary being. Nevertheless, the ontological argument does follow the right path, although in the wrong direction. That is why it cannot be dismissed without consideration, and why a consideration of it helps to clarify some fundamental notions.

The ontological argument, as presented in its simplest form by Descartes in the fifth of the *Metaphysical Meditations,* is the assertion that infinite being necessarily exists. To think of infinite being as dependent for its existence on something else would be absurd, for it would then be lacking in a possible perfection of being and would consequently be less than infinite. Hence the fact that we can think of infinite being is a guarantee that such a being exists.

The original argument of St. Anselm is not quite so

simply expressed.[1] St. Anselm takes as the current idea of God the being than which nothing greater can be thought; this, after all, is merely another way of stating the infinity of being which we attribute to God. But, St. Anselm urges, it would be contradictory to suppose that such a being exists only in the form of a concept in the mind, for in that case we could conceive of something greater, namely the same being but as existing also in fact. Hence the notion of the greatest of all thinkable beings entails its real existence.

Although St. Bonaventure is content to reproduce this reasoning as it stands,[2] Duns Scotus is, as usual, rather more subtle. The Anselmian argument might suggest that an actually existent infinite being was greater as an object of thought than one which existed only in the mind. This would be open to the Kantian objection that there are no more dollars in a hundred real dollars than there are in a hundred possible dollars. Scotus points out that it would be erroneous to suppose that anything is greater as an object of thought merely because it also exists; the crucial consideration is that what really exists is a greater being than anything that is only an object of thought. *Non sic intelligendo quod idem, si cogitetur, per hoc sit maius cogitabile si existat; sed omni quod est in intellectu tantum est maius aliquod cogitabile quod existit.*[3]

Moreover Scotus adds to the argument a precision which Descartes later did not see to be needed. The reasoning can stand only if we can see that infinite being is possible or non-contradictory; if it were a contradiction in terms, nothing that we could say about it would have any real validity. But Scotus is satisfied that no contradiction is

[1] St. Anselm: *Proslogion*, Cap. 2–3.
[2] St. Bonaventure: *Quaestio Disputata de Mysterio Trinitatis*, qu. 1, art. i.
[3] Duns Scotus: *De Primo Principio*, cap. iv, no. 25.

involved in the notion of infinite being. If there were, it would be strange that nobody had so far been able to point it out. In reality the notion of infinite being presents itself to us as, absolutely speaking, the ideal of perfect intelligibility. *Intellectus, cuius obiectum est ens, nullam invenit repugnantiam intelligendo ens infinitum; imo videtur perfectissimum intelligibile.*[1]

Scotus's clarification of St. Anselm's argument can be paralleled by Leibniz's comments upon Descartes. Already in the early *Discours de Métaphysique*, Leibniz maintained the ontological argument in the form that, if God is possible, he necessarily exists.[2] In the *Monadology*, he amplifies his thought by the consideration that only limits or negations can be a source of contradiction.[3] The being in which there is no limit or negation must, therefore, be intrinsically possible. But, if God is possible, he necessarily exists. Hence God exists.

2

This argument is commonly criticized on the ground that it jumps from the logical to the real order, from a mere concept to an existent thing. The criticism is valid, but it requires explanation, for in this form it simply contradicts the principle of the argument. The adherents of the ontological argument maintain precisely that in at least one case, and indeed in only one case, it is legitimate to reason from concept to fact. Since it is not immediately evident that this is universally false, they can be refuted only by a frontal attack on their specific argument, or by a demonstration that it is never possible to reason from concept to fact.

---

[1] *Loc. cit.*
[2] Leibniz: *Discours de Métaphysique*, § 23.
[3] Leibniz: *Monadology*, § 45.

St. Thomas insists that our knowledge of the divine nature is not sufficiently clear and direct to enable us to affirm immediately that God exists. If we had a direct knowledge of God, we should perceive at once that he necessarily exists, for his essence and his existence are one. Hence the proposition that God exists must be allowed to be immediately evident in itself, but it is not immediately evident to us, who form our notion of God from inadequate concepts derived from created things. We must, therefore, employ reasoning in order to arrive at a knowledge of God's existence.[1]

What are we to say to those who, like Scotus and Leibniz, maintain that, although our knowledge of the divine nature is obviously inadequate, it is nevertheless sufficient to entitle us to affirm that an infinite being is intrinsically possible, and that the intrinsic possibility of an infinite and, consequently, necessary being is a sufficient guarantee of its actual existence? We must consider what we mean when we say that something is possible. In general, intrinsic possibility means the absence of contradiction; it means that the elements which make up the concept of the thing are compatible. A circle one foot in diameter is possible; a square circle is contradictory and impossible. There is, however, an evident difference between the case in which we know all the essential notes of a thing and the case in which we do not. In the former case intrinsic possibility acquires an absolute sense; in the latter it means only that, as far as we know, the thing is possible or that we do not see it to be impossible. It can be granted that we perceive no incompatibility of the notion of being with the notion of unlimited perfection. But our notions of infinity and, especially, of being are so

---

[1] St. Thomas Aquinas: *Summa contra Gentiles*, I, 10–11, and *Summa Theologica*, I, qu. 2, art. i.

inadequate to all that they might contain, that we are certainly not entitled to say in advance that infinite being involves in itself no element of contradiction; we can say only that we perceive no contradiction, that, as far as we know, such a being is possible. Hence we require grounds other than its mere notion to enable us to assert its real existence.

In any case, what is it that we are asserting when we say that infinite being necessarily exists? Kant raised this more radical question with his denial that existence is a predicate. For of what can existence be predicated? However we may manipulate grammatical subjects and grammatical predicates, a logical subject is presupposed to its predicate. When we say that something exists, the subject may be interpreted as the concept of the thing. If so, we are asserting only that the concept exists and are saying nothing of any real thing corresponding with it. If, on the other hand, the subject is the real existent thing, we are asserting nothing new by saying that it exists. When, therefore, we state that infinite being exists, we are either begging the question by assuming a real infinite being as subject or saying only that the concept of infinite being exists. In neither case will this serve as evidence for the existence of infinite being, and we can see in general that it is impossible by beginning with mere concepts to end with anything save mere concepts. That is why it is impossible to argue from the logical to the real order.[1]

The genuine purport of the principle of the ontological argument becomes still clearer if we see that it is intended to be an entailment. When we express it in hypothetical form, it becomes the statement: If infinite being exists, it exists necessarily. This is perfectly true and evident, but

<hr />

[1] Kant: *Kritik der reinen Vernunft.* " Von der Unmöglichkeit eines ontologischen Beweises vom Dasein Gottes," A 592–602, B 620–30.

it is equally evident that such a premiss is of no help in showing that infinite being actually exists. It is important, however, to notice that the objection to the principle of the ontological argument is not that it is false but that, when properly understood, it is useless for the purpose for which it is put forward.

3

Since the notion of an infinite being does not warrant the assertion of its actual existence, we must proceed in the reverse direction and, having shown that some necessary being exists, go on to show that such a being can only be infinite. Kant objects that we cannot do this without becoming enmeshed in the ontological argument. For, he says, if the proposition that all necessary being is infinite is subjected to the process of logical conversion, it becomes the proposition that some infinite being is necessary. Since, however, there can by definition be only one infinite being, some infinite being is equivalent to all infinite being. Hence the proposition that some infinite being is necessary can be replaced by the proposition that all infinite being is necessary, which is the principle of the ontological argument. You cannot, therefore, assert that necessary being is infinite without equivalently embracing the ontological argument.

This need not perturb us if we remember that the objection to the principle of the ontological argument is not that it is false but that it does not serve to prove the existence of God. Since it is true that, if infinite being exists, it exists necessarily, we should not be embarrassed, even were the statement that, if there is a necessary being this is infinite, reducible to it.

In reality, moreover, Kant's attempted reduction is fallacious, for it involves the unwarranted and contradictory assumption of an existential import for the particular proposition that some infinite being is necessary. It is only if at least one infinite being *must* be necessary that the fact that there can be only one infinite being entails that this infinite being is necessary. In the context, however, the statement that some infinite being is necessary means, not that at least one infinite being is necessary, but that infinite being *may* be necessary.

When the whole argument is rephrased in the more appropriate terms of intension rather than in misleading terms of extension, Kant's mistake becomes clear. If necessity entails infinity, it follows that infinity is compatible with necessity. But nothing more follows; even though there can be only one infinite being, and even if this infinite being were not necessary, it might still be true that infinity was abstractly compatible with necessity. Hence it cannot be inferred that infinity entails necessity. We think, indeed, that both statements are true; we think that, if there is an infinite being, it exists necessarily, and that, if there is a necessary being, it is infinite. Nevertheless these are logically independent truths.

We must now make good the contention that necessary being must be infinite. This proposition becomes evident when we grasp the notion of being adequately. Being, as Kant rightly says, is not a logical predicate. There is no subject which remains the same in itself while existence may be given to it or not; there is no independent world of essences waiting to be called into existence. Either they exist in.some sense already, which would be a contradiction, or they are no more than ideas in a mind able to entertain their possibility and, maybe, to realize them.

When we consider the relationship between being and the forms of being, we find that, since all the forms of being obviously presuppose being itself, we must look upon being as a subject. When we say that a black swan exists, we are not adding existence to the concept of a black swan; the concept existed already as a concept in the mind, and it is not a constituent of the black swan which exists in fact. What we mean, therefore, may be more precisely rendered by the statement that something takes the form of a black swan. Being is a subject to which the qualities of a black swan can be attributed.

We are not here adopting Bradley's view that every judgment has the same ultimate subject, which is the whole system of reality. For the completely universal notion of being is also inseparable from individuality. All the forms which being can take are capable of being conceptually assimilated in abstraction and of being potentially attributed to many individuals. No doubt it is possible to make an exclusive description of a thing in terms of essence as opposed to existence, but such a description does not designate the absolute individuality of the thing, for the elements out of which it is composed are attributable to more things than one. It is precisely when we think of a thing as an existent that its individuality presents itself directly to mind. Hence the view that being is the ultimate subject is so far from leading to monism that it is rather the only adequate means of avoiding monism. Philosophies which neglect the notion of existence are logically inclined towards monism; philosophies which emphasize existence must be pluralistic.

Existence is not a concept like other concepts, because it is presented to us only in the act of judgment. It represents in the first place, therefore, that aspect of knowledge by which knowledge is experience. When we say *This is a tree* or *This is a flower* or *This is a fruit*, the nature of tree or flower or fruit is something which we conceptually assimilate to ourselves, but *This is* is an unique element which represents the fact that we are having experience, and the *This* is inseparable from the *Is*. Because we can say *This is somewhat*, we are not merely spinning a web of concepts, but are in contact with a world.

When we reflect on this unique notion of existence, we discover it to be the fundamental energy by which things are what they are. Being is not a pale receptacle of the forms of being, for these, in so far as they are positive, are themselves being. The nature of being as fundamental subject is not closed but open; it passes over into and includes what is positive in the forms of being. The forms of being as we know them in distinction from being itself are specified rather as the limitations within which the nature of being is realized in ourselves and in our experience. It is not because they are beings that this being is this kind of being and that being is that kind of being; the nature of being is constrained to the limits within which we find it.[1]

How, then, must we think of necessary being? It can only be being unconstrained, being unlimited. When being takes this limited form or that, we have always to ask why it does so and to look for a cause beyond the thing itself. The nature of being, when we consider it absolutely, is equally positively related to all that is positive in the forms of being. Hence everything finite demands a cause; the uncaused or necessary being must be infinite, uniting in itself the whole positive perfection of which being is capable.

It should be noted that we cannot, on a par with the ontological argument, argue simply from the nature of being to the existence of infinite being, for we do not know

[1] For a fuller presentation of this line of thought, see my article on "The Anatomy of Existence" in the *Dublin Review*, Oct. 1946.

a priori that a being uniting in itself the whole perfection of being is intrinsically possible and does not involve contradiction. What we know is that, if there is a necessary being, this must be an infinite being. We have learned already that, if anything exists, necessary being exists. We know by experience that something exists. Hence we can infer that necessary being exists and that there is only one necessary being, for necessary being is infinite being.

4

This line of thought about being is one which emerges into explicitness for the first time in the work of St. Thomas Aquinas, and we shall not be going too far in saying that it constitutes his most compelling claim to philosophical eminence. Moreover we have, in reading St. Thomas, the interest of seeing it in process of emergence, for he inherited from Avicenna a rather different view of being and only gradually established his own improved point of view. Avicenna deserves the credit for having given to the notion of being the importance which it merits in philosophy, but he does not transcend a conception of being which would make it, in Kantian terms, a logical and metaphysical predicate. His is the mode of speech according to which essences either receive existence or not, and this, if its literal significance is pressed, is open to the same objection as the ontological argument.

In the *De Ente et Essentia* we find the youthful Aquinas speaking like Avicenna. Essences are described as being intelligible apart from existence and as either receiving existence or not. If anything receives existence, it must receive it from a cause. Hence it cannot be true that everything has an essence which receives existence, or there would be an infinite causal regress. There must, consequently, be something whose essence is identical with existence, and this is God.[1] This language has not been without its influence on later Thomists, but it is certainly objectionable on the score that the essence which receives existence, and is in itself indifferent to existence, is a myth. There is all the difference in the world between the mere idea of a thing and the nature of a really existent thing.

St. Thomas, while he continues on occasion to employ Avicennian language, supplies in other passages of his later works the necessary corrective. The Fourth Way of the *Summa Theologica*, which has its counterpart in the *Summa contra Gentiles*, is, as it is expressed in these two works, scarcely more than an assertion that there must be something which is *maxime ens*, something which unites the whole perfection of being. The reasoning upon which this conclusion depends is to be found in the detailed arguments by which St. Thomas shows that there can be no metaphysical composition in necessary being, that it must be pure act and being itself, and that it must contain the perfection of all things.

The most characteristic argument of St. Thomas for this final conclusion is that, " since God is subsistent being itself, nothing of the perfection of being can be wanting in him. The perfections of all things are contained in the perfection of being, for things are perfect in so far as they possess a degree of being; whence it follows that God does not lack the perfection of anything."[2] What is the notion of being which this passage enforces? It is certainly not the

---

[1] St. Thomas Aquinas: *De Ente et Essentia*, cap. v (iii). Cf. F. Van Steenberghen in *Revue Philosophique de Louvain*, 1947, pp. 161–3. His three articles on " Le Problème Philosophique de l'Existence de Dieu ", although unduly severe in places on the traditional language, should be read by all who aim at a critically adequate natural theology.

[2] St. Thomas Aquinas: *Summa Theologica*, I, qu. 4, art. ii.

notion of a bare existence which may or may not be added to the variegated potentialities of essence; it is the notion of a fundamental energy which is the source of all that is positive in essence itself. An Avicennian essence is all that an existing thing is except the little detail of existence; in this new account essence, as distinct from existence, becomes merely the boundary which limits the bursting energy of being.[1]

If what we have previously said in this chapter is true, this is a Thomistic innovation of the first importance, and it casts a retrospective light upon what St. Thomas says of metaphysical composition and its absence in God. By metaphysical composition is meant a tension between a factor of positivity which is potentially unlimited within its order and a factor of limitation. With what we may now call St. Thomas's own theory of being, the distinction between essence and existence is not simply a distinction of an essence which does not demand existence and the existence which may or may not be conferred upon it; this is open to the objections constantly urged by the opponents of the distinction, when they ask what can be meant by an essence apart from existence. The distinction is really a tension between the positive energy of being, which of itself knows no limits, and the limitations within which being is realized in this finite thing or that. When being is thus realized within the bounds of a finite essence, it must always be contingent and caused. Necessary being can contain no such tension; it must be pure actuality and pure being, and that is infinite being.

It may be added that, although Duns Scotus's notion of being is a much poorer one than that of St. Thomas, he is

---

[1] For this interpretation of St. Thomas, cf. E. Gilson: *God and Philosophy*, pp. 62–73.

at one with his predecessor in perceiving infinity as God's fundamental mode of being. Infinity, says Scotus, is not like an attribute or a relative character, such as are even the transcendental notions of truth and goodness. It is an intrinsic mode of being, and precisely the intrinsic mode of the necessary and divine being; from it can be deduced the attributes of God.

We have tried in this chapter to present the notion of being in such a way that the equation of necessary with infinite being may become evident. For this purpose the concept of a bare existence which applies in the same way to everything that exists and is bestowed upon selected members of a shadow-world of possible essences must be transcended. Being must be conceived with a logical priority to the limitations within which we find it realized in finite things, and must be seen of itself to involve no limit to the fullness of its realization. If, then, there is a necessary being, which is being of itself, this is an infinite being. But there must be a necessary being. Therefore there is an infinite being, and this is God.

CHAPTER VI

ETERNAL MIND

I

GOD is the infinite fullness of being; he includes in the unity of his nature all the perfections which are to be found in a finite degree among his creatures. Yet no one is likely to want to assert that God is corporeal. This means that we instinctively acknowledge that nothing corporeal could be all-perfect and that to be corporeal is a mode of imperfection. If we express this in more metaphysical terms, it means that, although nothing can be without some perfection or actuality, what precisely makes a thing corporeal is a mode of not-being. In other words, we instinctively acknowledge the truth of hylomorphism.

What, after all, distinguishes a body from what is incorporeal? The essential difference is between what is extended in three dimensions and what is unextended. But to be extended in three dimensions is to be less one and, therefore, less perfect than to be unextended. Let it not be objected that this makes a point more perfect than a volume. A point is merely an ideal limit which has no reality in itself and pertains to reality only in so far as it is a limit of something extended. Hence a point does not enter into a comparison of real perfection. What we are saying is that to be real without that dissipation of existence which is spatial extension is to be more perfect than anything corporeal.

Moreover the character of extension is to contain not only a potential multiplicity of parts but a potential infinity of parts. Whatever may be physically possible, it is absolutely conceivable that anything extended should be divided indefinitely. A potential infinity of division is at the opposite extreme from an actual infinity of perfection. It is an element of unintelligibility in the sense that its intelligibility consists exclusively in the negation of the absolute intelligibility of unity. It implies, consequently, a principle of pure potentiality in the order of essence, which is what Aristotle and St. Thomas meant by first matter. We cannot understand philosophically the nature of body without perceiving in it this duality of the pure potentiality of first matter and the element of form which makes a body to be what it actually is.

A full discussion of the metaphysics of the corporeal belongs elsewhere; so much is introduced here in order to remind us of why we cannot conceive of God as corporeal. For God is the fullness of being and pure actuality without any admixture of potentiality. But anything corporeal contains a principle of pure potentiality. Therefore God is not corporeal.

A little more explanation is necessary before we can speak confidently of God as mind. We have to see first that the general notion of mind, unlike that of body, is not necessarily of something finite. We have to see that mind in itself is a pure perfection which does not imply any element of incompleteness or potentiality. Only if this is true can we assert literally that God is mind. Otherwise we should have, like the Neoplatonists, to assert that the first principle is above mind as above matter.

We consider mind in so far as we have direct experience of it, and that is of our own minds. Here we notice many elements of imperfection. The range of our minds is limited, and not only is it limited in fact but it is limited in principle, for we are dependent upon the material provided by sensation and reflection. Our direct knowledge is of a very restricted field; we are often reduced to reasoning from one thing to another, and only rarely does our reasoning attain to absolute certainty. Our intellectual life is a succession of limited views, in which the clear apprehension of one set of objects is impossible unless we leave others out of consideration.

Think what mind would be without these limitations. Let us conceive of a mind whose range is unlimited, for it has a direct knowledge of everything that is, and in which there is no succession of limited views, for it is aware of everything at once. Is there in such a mind any element of imperfection? We must answer in the negative. Mind is in itself a pure perfection of being, for, in contrast with mere being, it is a being which possesses itself fully by awareness of itself and possesses things other than itself in a unique way by awareness of them. Limitation of range and successiveness of perspective, such as we discover in our own minds, are accidental to the general nature of mind. Consequently, to the infinite being who is God we can literally attribute the character of mind in its full and pure perfection as an unchanging awareness of itself and of all that is and can be. God is eternal mind.

2

We must, however, linger on the notion of eternity, for this aspect of the divine being, so positive as it must be in itself, can be known by us only dimly and negatively. We do not find it so difficult to think of God as incorporeal and superior to spatial extension, for we possess in our own thinking an incorporeal factor and can readily see how this is superior to our embodiment. But we are altogether, body and mind, in time, and we have no positive analogue by which to conceive a superiority to temporal duration and succession.

Nevertheless, when we reflect on temporal duration, we see that it is in itself a mode of not-being, a mode of the dissipation of existence. Spatial extension is the specific mode of not-being characteristic of the material world; a stretched-out duration is a mode of not-being which attaches to all finite things, all things whose essence is not the fullness of existence, all things ·which have potential natures to be fulfilled in collaboration with circumstances and to be fulfilled gradually. We can see that it pertains to absolute perfection to exist fully all at once and not successively, but fatally, when we try to conceive this positively, we are thrown back on the totally misleading analogy of a moment of time. We try to conceive eternity and can only think of a duration without beginning and without end; we correct this by eliminating the successiveness of duration, and we find that we are thinking only of momentariness.

Boethius made clearly the necessary distinction between perpetuity and eternity, invoking the assistance of Plato in the *Timaeus*. For Plato the Forms or Ideas are " immutably selfsame ", having no succession of phases of existence, and the Demiurge, in shaping a world which will not cease to exist, makes it " a moving likeness of everlastingness ", having a duration without end.[1] The theist Boethius attributes eternity not simply to the Forms but to God; it is God who is immutably selfsame, enjoying in his eternity the simultaneous and perfect possession of endless life (*interminabilis vitae tota simul et perfecta possessio*). In so far as

[1] Plato: *Timaeus*, 37C–38B. The quoted phrases are from A. E. Taylor's translation (London, Methuen, 1929, p. 34).

things created by God may always be conserved by him in being and never have an end to their duration, this duration, inevitably remaining a successiveness, may be described, in distinction from eternity, as perpetuity.[1]

Our difficulty, then, is that, when we try to think of eternity, we are always tempted to think of it as perpetuity, as a duration without limit. But the divine eternity must be something much more positive than perpetuity. The divine eternity is so positive that it excludes the successiveness which is implied by perpetuity. There can be no before or after in God, for this implies a changeability which is incompatible with necessary and perfect being. God can only be conceived as superior to the dissipation of time as he is superior to the dissipation of space. He does not exist at a moment any more than he exists at a point; his being has a positivity which transcends time as much as it transcends space. While we have in our own minds a positive analogue by which we can conceive the transcendence of space, we have no such positive analogue by which to conceive the transcendence of time. We are left with a purely negative concept which we know to connote something unknown which is eminently positive, but it is a compensation that this is enough for us, since we are genuinely capable of thinking and not merely imagining. By this tenuous thread we can conceive and affirm the divine eternity in which there is no changeability and no succession, no before or after, but a simultaneous infinity of being and knowing.

God, then, is eternal mind, exempt from succession as he is exempt from extension, unchangeably contemplating his own being and all that can be derived from it. He has no need of anything other than himself; his being is satisfied

[1] Boethius: *De Consolatione Philosophiae*, lib. V, pr. 6.

in the possession of its own fullness. Creation is not to be explained by any need of God; it can only be explained by the divine generosity. God in himself, since he is infinite being, must be the eternal fullness of thought.

3

St. Augustine, making use of the Platonic tradition, reasons more directly than St. Thomas to the existence of an eternal mind.[1] He contrasts the contingent and changing objects of perception with the necessary and unchanging objects of thought. The things of experience exist in time, coming into being and passing away, but the intelligible aspects which we find in them are outside time; they may be verified at any time and they preserve their essential truth even when they are unverified. Augustine is especially impressed by those ideas which are at the same time ideals incompletely verified in the things of experience. Exact numerical proportions are scarcely to be found in nature; one thing is only approximately twice the size of another. Nevertheless the mathematical laws by which we judge the things of experience, have an exactness and a certainty by which they belong to a different order from the things to which they are applied. So also is it with wisdom, which is the intellectual apprehension of the supreme good, and of the goodness of the rest in relation to it. Here we conceive and seek after something which is only imperfectly participated in the things of experience.

When we are fully in the realm of thought, therefore, we are in contact with a system of truth which is timelessly valid and equally valid for all minds. Since our minds are

---

[1] The principal references for St. Augustine's argument are to his *De Libero Arbitrio*, Bk. II, and *De Vera Religione*, cc. 29–31.

in themselves individual and temporal, this means that we are participating in a truth which is superior to us. " Nor is it to be doubted that the unchangeable nature, which is superior to the rational soul, is God, and that the primal life and the primal essence coincide with the primal wisdom. For this is that unchangeable truth which is rightly described as the law of all arts and the art of the almighty artificer."[1] It is by the light which God communicates to our minds that we apprehend eternal and necessary truths, and by our recognition of this that we come to a knowledge of God, the eternal and infinite mind.

This typically Augustinian argument has scarcely received sufficient attention. At times it seems almost to have been lost to sight, for Norris of Bemerton, advancing essentially the same form of reasoning in " A Metaphysical Essay toward the Demonstration of a God, from the Steddy and Immutable nature of Truth ",[2] claims that " 'tis no where universally receiv'd, nor by any that I know of industriously and pro-fessedly managed ". Before considering its logical value, let us rephrase it a little.

Our awareness of *particular* things and the propositions which we formulate about them, present an evident contrast with our apprehension of *universals* and the necessary propositions which enunciate relationships between uni-versals. In the former case the objects of our thought exist in time and truths about them are temporally conditioned; in the latter case we are apprehending natures which may be verified at any time and propositions whose truth is timeless. Peter exists in time, and Peter walks for a period of time; the essential nature of man is the same at all times and would have been the same to any mind which could

---

[1] St. Augustine: *De Vera Religione*, c. 31.
[2] John Norris: *Miscellanies*, ed. 2 (1692), pp. 193–207.

conceive it, even if men had never existed. The statement that man is a rational animal is true of all men and is ideally true in independence of the existence of any man.

From the apprehension of universal concepts and of truths about them which are the same for all minds and at all times the Augustinian argument infers the existence of an eternal mind which timelessly contemplates the eternal truth in which we imperfectly participate. A likely objection to this inference is that concepts are not realities apart from minds and that the proper form of necessary propositions is hypothetical. Even if the concept of man is the same for all minds at all times, it is only in the hypothesis that a mind exists that the concept may be formed at all. If there is a mind which conceives of man, it will conceive of him as a rational animal and will judge that, if there is a man, he is a rational animal, but this does not entitle us to assert that such a mind eternally exists.

Perhaps there is a latent premiss in the Augustinian argument which overcomes this difficulty. This latent premiss will include precisely the factor of existence, whose explicit acknowledgment is Thomistic rather than Augustinian. For truth is eventually correspondence with fact; even hypothetical truth is based upon actual fact and is finally justified by actual fact. We have to ask whether the contingent and changing facts which are the objects of our experience provide an adequate foundation for the timeless and necessary truths which we come to know by abstraction from them. The answer, upon reflection, is negative. If all reality were irremediably temporal and contingent, truth could have no superior prerogative; all truths would equally be contingent and temporally conditioned. Since we apprehend timeless and necessary truths, and since all the characters of truth eventually rest upon correspondence with fact, there must be in fact itself something eternal and necessary.

This line of thought, moreover, enables us to say at once of what sort eternal and necessary reality must be. For things and their relationships are contingent and temporal; what is eternal and necessary consists in their ideal natures and the relationships between them. Hence eternal and necessary being is a mind contemplating in itself the possibilities of existence and the laws which govern it. Reflection upon our intellectual activities shows us the trace of timeless necessity and makes us discover its source in the existence of eternal mind as the primal fact and the origin of all other fact. The Augustinian argument, when its latent premiss of the dependence of truth in its whole character upon existent fact is made explicit, is valid; it shows the existence of eternal mind by the way in which our own minds participate in it.

4

If St. Augustine's argument was not always and everywhere received, it survived at any rate in that particular application of it which is the teleological argument. In saying this we have set ourselves the task not only of expounding the teleological argument but also of showing that it is a form of the general inference to eternal mind. The Fifth Way of the *Summa Theologica*, which is parallel to the last argument for the existence of God in the *Summa contra Gentiles*, reasons from the order of the world to a supreme intelligence which is its source. For even those things which lack mind act purposefully, and tend towards a determinate fulfilment; their activity is not fortuitous but shows a constant pattern. Since purposeful activity is characteristic of mind, and since these are agents which lack mind, there must be a mind which directs them and communicates their finality to them. This supreme intelligence is God.

Kant treats this argument with respect but points out that it is incomplete by itself, for, even if the inference were allowed to be certain, it would arrive only at an architect and not at a creator of the world. In order to establish the existence of a creator we must invoke the cosmological argument, and, according to Kant, the cosmological presupposes the ontological argument. Hence, while the teleological argument remains suggestive and persuasive, it cannot claim to be an adequate speculative foundation for belief in God.

Before taking up a position in relation to Kant we must make the argument more explicit. It has, indeed, been developed in more than one way. In a rather naïve form it has sometimes been presented as an argument for the fundamental goodness of the universe and, consequently, for the existence of a benevolent power. How is it that we and the other species of things which inhabit the world, dependent as we are on external conditions for our development and survival, find what we require in our environment? Must it not be an all-wise and all-good God who has arranged the world in this way? The obvious retort is that, if our environment did not in general contain what is needed for survival, we should not have survived at all. The world happens to be suited to our survival, although it may be such as to inhibit the development of unimagined species far worthier than ourselves. The Darwinian doctrine of the survival of the fittest, although far from being a satisfactory universal explanation of cosmic development, is at any rate a considerable objection to the more naïve forms of the teleological argument.

It may be observed in general that to attempt to argue to the goodness of the universe before establishing the existence of a good God is a rash enterprise. Our knowledge of the world is far too limited to provide us with sufficient material for such an argument. If this discussion is conducted without assuming theism, the disputants are likely to arrive at different conclusions according to the state of their digestions and their opinions about the trend of contemporary history. At the present period of history especially, no very satisfactory outcome is to be expected.

A more serious form of the teleological argument is derived from the observation of organic facts. In organisms, particles of matter are combined in what, absolutely speaking, is an extremely improbable way in order to form self-maintaining, self-developing and self-propagating systems. It seems altogether too much of a coincidence to suppose that, if no mind had formed the world and presided over its history, matter would of itself have found these combinations. Yet, since this is one possible form of the combination of material particles among an uncountable number, and since any combination has the same intrinsic probability as any other, we cannot on such grounds absolutely exclude the possibility that the world has just happened to be what it is. If there were originally nothing but evolving particles of matter, the most likely resultant world would be a chaos, but we cannot therefore exclude the possibility of a less likely resultant world which would possess the characters of the world in which we live. If this amount of coincidence seems too unplausible, we might fall back on the hypothesis of a latent life-force in matter which has gradually revealed itself in the course of history. This is a much less intelligible theory than theism, but it cannot be refuted by the sort of fact which we are at present considering.

All these suppositions have a somewhat vertiginous effect, for they are really possible only when we leave out of account what is most essential and most central. The point is not that the universe at once manifests a fundamental goodness or that it contains what are, absolutely speaking, extremely improbable combinations of material particles; the point is much simpler. It is that the universe manifests any order at all. It does not matter whether we regard the laws of the behaviour of things as helpful or as sinister, as intrinsically likely or as intrinsically unlikely; it is sufficient that we recognize that everything in the world does act in accordance with general laws. As a thing is, so it acts. Our knowledge of physical laws is limited and approximate, but we know enough to be able to say that intelligible general rules are applicable to the behaviour of things which lack intelligence, at least as much as to the behaviour of those which possess it.

This is the really overwhelming realization, or it would be if we were not so used to it, and it can be if we see the matter afresh. The whole realm of fact, including even what is farthest removed from mind, completely individual and subject to time as it is, exhibits a system of intelligible and timeless universal relationships. All truth must be founded on fact, but mindless fact is no sufficient foundation for universal characters and universal laws. We are bound to infer that reality primarily takes the form of eternal mind, contemplating in its own depths such characters and laws.

A similar remark applies to those who, like Newman, find their clearest source of conviction about God in the dictate of conscience as postulating " a Supreme Governor, a Judge, holy, just, powerful, all-seeing, retributive ".[1] If this be

---

[1] J. H. Newman, *Grammar of Assent*, Part I, ch. v, §1 (ed. 1924, p. 110).

understood as an argument attempting to establish the existence of a person from a feeling of obligation towards a person, it must be criticized as a reversal of logical order; a feeling of obligation towards a person presupposes a knowledge of the existence of the person. It would still be of interest as a biographical fact about Newman and others that the reality of God comes home to them with greatest force in connection with the sense of moral obligation. But, more than this, the absolute and universal character of moral law is one instance of the timeless truth with which we find ourselves in contact; hence the argument from conscience can be taken as another variant form of the Augustinian argument.

Kant's criticism of the teleological argument must, therefore, be criticized as not having penetrated to its deepest meaning, in which it appears as a form of the inference from timeless truth to an eternal mind. In its full generality this inference is typical of Augustine's approach. Some minds, however, have been especially impressed by those laws of nature which manifest what can only be called purposefulness in things which are devoid of the power of thought; in this case the inference becomes the teleological argument. Other minds have been mainly impressed by the absoluteness of moral law and have presented an argument from conscience. These lines of thought converge finally in the recognition of God as eternal mind.

CHAPTER VII

RETROSPECT AND PROSPECT

I

W E HAVE tried to make explicit a process of inference in which three steps can be distinguished. If anything exists, necessary being exists; necessary being must be infinite being; infinite being can only be eternal mind. But we know by experience that something exists. Hence there exists an infinite and eternal mind, which is God. When we look back upon this reasoning, an objection may occur which, in its simplest form, is the doubt whether we have not got out of our premisses more than is in them. The material of our thought is wholly derived from finite and temporal things; yet we have somehow got out of it the existence of an infinite and eternal being.

The conclusion of any useful inference, of course, must in a sense contain more than is in the premisses; it must contain something new, or our reasoning would merely be marking time. But, in saying this, we have not answered the objection completely. The objection is that we have arrived at a being of a wholly different order from the things with which we began. Must we not have made a logical, or illogical, jump somewhere? It is not like inferring about our new acquaintance Brown that he must have had parents, even though we have never met them or heard about them. Brown's parents are or were human beings of the same kind as himself. What we have now inferred is that the world had its origin in a being of a totally different kind from the things which make up the world.

Our problem, then, if we are to make the rationale of our argument clear, is to show that, while God is indeed of a different order from finite things, there is not such a total lack of community between the finite and the infinite as to invalidate an inference from one to the other. The answer to this problem is the doctrine of analogy. If the characters which we attribute to God had precisely the same significance for him that they have when attributed to finite things, we should merely have invented a finite god, and that is not God at all. If they had a completely different significance the word *God* would be as meaningless as abracadabra. The finding of the correct balance between these two impossible extremes is the work of arriving at a notion of analogy.

When two things are utterly different, they cannot have more than a fortuitous community of name. Thus well, as the adverb of good, and well, as meaning a source of water, have nothing in common but the name. This type of linguistic coincidence, although it is usually mentioned in connection with our subject, has no bearing upon it except by contrast. It is the case of purely verbal equivocation.

The approach to our real subject is better made from the other end, from the case of a similarity which is reducible to formal identity. Thus man, as applied to Peter, and man, as applied to Paul, have precisely the same meaning. An Englishman, a German, a Pole and a Jew are men in exactly the same sense. The mistake of the Nazis, if it can be reduced to a matter of logic, is to have supposed that Germans and non-Germans were not men in the same sense. Man, however, is a genuinely univocal term; it applies to all men in the same way.

There are other similarities, however, which are irreducible to formal identity in either of two ways. In the one case this irreducibility is due to a defect in our knowledge, since, although we know that there is both similarity and difference, we do not know precisely how far the similarity extends and where the difference begins. On the colloquial level we can often say that one thing is something like another, while we are unable to say how exactly it is like the other; thus kindly scientists, endeavouring to make their conclusions generally assimilable, used to inform us that the atom was something like a solar system and the brain something like a telephone exchange, although neither they nor we could ever make out exactly how far the analogy extended. In such cases it could often be assumed that, with more adequate knowledge, the vagueness would disappear, and we should be able to arrive at a formal identity and a precise difference. It is, however, possible to conceive a case in which human knowledge is in principle incapable of overcoming a certain vagueness and we must remain content with an analogy which is never completely reducible.

Similarity is also irreducible to formal identity in another type of instance, in which the irreducibility is completely objective. This is the case in which the nature of the factor itself is susceptible of degrees. Two sensations of heat are alike in being sensations of heat, but they may differ in their degree of heat. It is objectively impossible to isolate a general nature of hotness from a scale of degrees of heat, but it is equally clear that all sensations of heat have something in common. Hotness, then, is an objectively analogical factor, having in all its instances a real similarity which is objectively incapable of being isolated from the degrees in which it is manifested.

When we apply these general notions to our present subject, we find that being is objectively analogical in this latter sense. Existence is inconceivable except as the existence of something, and existence is proportionate to the essence which it realizes. Your existence is different from my existence, not only on account of the individual character which is inseparable from existence, but also because your existence is the realization of your powers, qualities and activities and my existence is the realization of my powers, qualities and activities. Hence the existences of different things have, so to say, different dimensions.

The being of God, since it is infinite being and the realization of the fullness of essential being which is identical with it, transcends any being of which we have experience. Nevertheless, as being, it has an analogical community with the being of even the poorest of finite things. The being of finite things is proportionate to their essences as the being of God is proportionate to his infinite essence. Consequently, since we are able to employ the notion of being, we are able validly to argue from the finite to the infinite and, although our conclusion so transcends our premises, our inference involves no logical hiatus. We are able to see that finite being entails infinite being because they are both being.

When, however, we attribute to God the positive perfections of essence, we find that an analogy of the former kind is involved. We know that all the positive perfections of being belong to God in their fullest form, but we have only finite perfections from which to argue. However much we strip away every element of imperfection that we can discern, we do not arrive at a positive conception of the infinite mode in which God possesses these perfections, and must be content with a residual imprecision. The attribute of eternity is a striking example. According to our capacity of thinking, eternity has to be conceived negatively as a mode of being without before or after. If this were all, we should conceive eternity in the same way as an indivisible moment in our experience. But we know that eternity must involve all that is positive in perpetual duration without being a duration. That, however, is all that we know. Eternity is like perpetual duration but has no before or after; eternity is like momentariness but at the opposite extreme of positivity. Our capacity of thinking can go no farther; we cannot define precisely where the similarity ends and the difference begins. We have to be content, when we try to think of the divine attributes, with analogical concepts whose imprecision is due to the imperfection of our own minds.

2

In the two *Summae*[1] St. Thomas dwells chiefly on a preliminary kind of verbal analogy which is usually described as the analogy of attribution. This occurs when the same term has two or more different but related meanings. Thus *healthy* refers in the first place to a condition of an organism, but it may be used to designate the kind of nourishment which conduces to health in the primary sense. God may be described by the names of whatever is of positive being and perfection in created things, for he is the cause of it.

But this is obviously not the whole story. St. Thomas insists also that there is a genuine similarity between the meanings in which the same term can be correctly applied both to God and to creatures.[2] If there were no such similarity, we should be saying nothing at all in applying to God a term which for us primarily designates some creaturely quality. Nevertheless we cannot maintain that it applies to God in

---

[1] Cf. St. Thomas Aquinas: *Summa Theologica*, I, qu. 13, art. v, and *Summa contra Gentiles*, I, 34.

[2] Cf. *Summa Theologica*, I, qu. 13, art. ii, and *Summa contra Gentiles*, I, 29.

precisely the same way as it applies to creatures, for the divine being in every respect infinitely exceeds anything finite. How, therefore, are we to understand this similarity?

In the *De Veritate*[1] St. Thomas throws out a suggestion which has been developed and systematized by later Thomists, especially by Cajetan. Here he says that, while there cannot be a proportion of the finite to the infinite, there can be within both the finite and the infinite proportions which are similar. Thus the divine goodness is to God as human goodness is to man, and the divine wisdom is to God as human wisdom is to man, and, in general, the divine attributes are to God as the analogous finite qualities are to finite things. This kind of analogy, which is a real and not merely a verbal analogy, is usually called the analogy of proportionality.

This suggestion is a helpful one. When we are appalled by the apparently unbridgeable distance between the finite and the infinite, we can reassure ourselves by a recognition of a genuine similarity of the ideal relationships on the one part and on the other. How can we conceive the infinite divine wisdom and goodness? At least we can perceive that there is a certain community between what it is for God to be wise and good and what it is for us to be wise and good.

Here again, nevertheless, we must acknowledge that the whole story has not been told. For the divine being and the divine attributes are not simply surds between which we recognize a relation similar to that of human nature to its positive perfections. If we are to say significantly that God is or that God is wise and good, there must be a certain absolute and not merely relative similarity of meaning between being, wisdom and goodness as applied to creatures and as applied to God. The relevant considerations have

[1] Cf. *De Veritate*, qu. 2, art. xi.

already been expressed. Existence has an absolute similarity of meaning, but it is in every case proportional to the forms of being within which it is realized. The positive perfections of being genuinely belong to God, but the mode of their presence in him so transcends the mode of their presence in finite things that we are unable to define where precisely the similarity ends and the difference begins. In spite of this we know, being armed with the transcendental notion of being, that there is a real community between God and creatures, and that what we say about God is so far from being meaningless that its real meaning is more positive than anything we can comprehend.

After this we can see what we mean by the simplicity of God. Metaphysical simplicity is contrasted with metaphysical composition. There cannot be in God any opposition or tension between different aspects of being such as there is in ourselves and other finite things. Everything that is necessarily verified in God implies, when its full purport is seen, everything else that is necessarily verified in God. This does not mean that all the terms which can be applied to God are really synonymous. They signify aspects of the divine being which are distinct for thought although they are not opposed in being. The truth is that they are aspects of a being which is wholly integrated in a sense of which the integration of human personality is the palest shadow. The better we understand any divine attribute, the more we see that it implies the others. The better we understand divine justice, the more we see that it implies divine mercy, and, the better we understand divine mercy, the more we see that it implies divine justice. The simplicity of God is not that of an undifferentiated homogeneity; it is a simplicity of complete harmony opposed to tension, opposition or composition but not, for us, to conceptual complexity.

3

The traditional methods of attaining a knowledge of the divine being are the *via affirmationis, via negationis,* and *via eminentiae.* These are not alternative methods or methods to be applied one by one but three factors to be observed in conjunction. God, says the Pseudo-Dionysius, whose cryptic formulae had so much influence on mediaeval thought, is " the affirmation of all, the negation of all, and that which is above every affirmation and negation".[1] That God is infinite being entails that we must affirm of him all that we know of the positive perfection of being, deny of him every limitation and imperfection, and attribute all perfections to him in a way which exceeds what we can positively conceive.

It is easy to see how we could lose a sense of the mystery of God by too exclusive an application of the way of affirmation. If we thought that we could come to know God adequately by an accumulation of self-contained and completely pellucid items of knowledge about him, we should be reducing him to our own level and thinking of him as if he were just another, although greater, finite thing. We have not to forget that the infinite belongs to a different order of being from the finite.

A more philosophical temptation is to apply too exclusively the way of negation. We have not now to consider the more radical agnosticism which holds that we can never be certain whether God exists or not; there is also a less radical but quite real agnosticism which holds that, although we know that there is a God, we cannot trust ourselves to say anything definite about him. Its chief mediaeval representative, countered by St. Thomas, was the Jewish thinker Moses Maimonides, who so emphasized the divine transcendence

[1] Pseudo-Dionysius: *De Divinis Nominibus,* ii, 4.

that he left us with nothing to attribute to God but the causation of the world and the negation of the qualities to be found in created things. In modern times the truly religious philosophy of Sir William Hamilton placed God, under the title of the Unconditioned, so absolutely beyond finite categories that we could have no really positive knowledge of his attributes; the Unknowable of Herbert Spencer was rather a perfunctory acknowledgment of a being beyond the world who was too remote to need to be taken into account. Such ways of thinking have had much influence on the ordinary educated modern mind; there are plenty of people who, while admitting that God exists, dispense themselves from thinking about him on the score that it would be unprofitable to do so, for he is too far beyond the capacities of human thought.

To such people we must recall the validity of the way of affirmation, based as it is on the all-embracing notion of being, and at the same time admitting the necessity of the way of negation, show that the two combined result in the way of eminence by which we attribute to God not a lesser but a greater positivity than we can adequately conceive. By the analogy of being we can justify our proof of God's existence and our affirmation of the divine attributes. In all that we have said and shall say about God we must be understood as implying the ways of affirmation, negation and eminence. Our statements about him can be wholly true although inadequate, and a residue of greater reality than we are able to utter must always be understood behind them.

CHAPTER VIII

CREATION

I

G OD, as the sole necessary being, must be the source of any other beings that exist. His power is, in the strict sense, creative; it does not, like the powers of created things, presuppose a material out of which things can be made, but is a power to call things into being out of nothingness by a mere act of will. Whatever is in itself possible must be possible of creation by God. We do not, however, have to say that God could call into being what is intrinsically contradictory, such as a square circle or a nullification of the past. The intrinsically contradictory is radically impossible in itself, and it is no limitation upon the power of the Almighty to say that God cannot produce the meaningless. The rationality of the universe is grounded in the nature of God, and the divine will cannot contradict the divine nature. So much may suffice today, when the question is no longer an actual one, for the gratuitous suppositions of Ockham and Descartes about what might be possible by the arbitrary will of God. Their mistake was to think of God as a will in priority to an intellect. But intellect is essentially prior to will; God is, first, eternal mind and, therefore, rational will.

A more perennial question is whether God is free to create or not. We have a natural reluctance to admit that we might never have existed at all, for each one of us feels that the universe would have been somehow incomplete

without him. This non-rational feeling has often been trans-
lated into philosophical terms as a necessity to create on the
part of God. Such a view is commonly associated with some
approximation towards pantheism, like the far from clear
ancient doctrine of the origin of things by emanation from
God rather than creation in the strict sense. So, in modern
times, the Hegelians hold that God is not more necessary
to the world than the world is to God. In so far as the background of this opinion is pantheistic or semi-pantheistic, it
is excluded by the absolute distinction which we must
evidently acknowledge between the finite and the infinite.

On a theistic basis Malebranche and Leibniz come to
mind as having asserted that God is necessitated by his own
nature to create the actual world as being the best of all
possible worlds. Leibniz's reasoning in the *Monadology*
is so brief and clear that it may be reproduced.

Since the divine ideas contain an infinite multitude of
possible worlds, and only one of these can exist, there must
be a sufficient reason which determines God to choose one
rather than another. This reason can be found only in the
appropriateness arising out of the degrees of perfection
found in these possible worlds, each laying claim to existence
in proportion to the perfection that it contains. This
consequently, is the cause of the existence of the best possible
world known to God by his wisdom, chosen by him on
account of his goodness, and brought into being by his
power.[1]

Our first point, which is not a difficult one, is that God has
no need of the world. Nothing can be wanting to infinite
being, and an infinite and eternal mind must find complete
satisfaction in itself. Hence the world adds nothing to God,

[1] Leibniz: *Monadology*, §§ 53–5.

and there is nothing about the world which could necessitate God to create it.

The suggestion that the divine nature is essentially creative is more serious. It might well be thought, as it has been thought, that, in accordance with the old maxim that good is diffusive of itself, the divine goodness could not but overflow into the act of creation. Yet, when we reflect, we must acknowledge that personal goodness does not automatically and necessarily diffuse itself. It belongs to the degree of perfection possessed by a person that he is in some measure the master of his activities, and, the more completely he possesses the perfection of personality, the more he is the master of his activities. A personal God must possess the perfection of personality in the highest degree and must, consequently, be thought of as utterly free in his external activity. While it is appropriate that God should manifest himself in creation, we must hold that he is in no way necessitated to do so.

Nor, if he creates, is God bound to create one possible world rather than another. When Malebranche and Leibniz speak of the best of all possible worlds, it is not at all clear that this expression makes sense. Any world that God created would be created with perfect wisdom and goodness and would manifest the infinite wisdom and goodness of God. But this would be true whatever things the world contained, and it does not follow that God had to create these actual things rather than others. Moreover, when we consider created things individually, we must admit with St. Thomas that God could have conferred upon them greater perfection than he did.[1] God could have produced a human race consisting entirely of eminent philosophers, and we may perhaps be grateful that he did not. On the

---

[1] St. Thomas Aquinas: *Summa Theologica*, I, qu. 25, art. vi.

supposition, however, that these things and not others were created, St. Thomas points out that the good of the universe, in so far as it consists in order and final harmony, could not have been greater. *Universum, suppositis istis rebus, non potest esse melius propter decentissimum ordinem his rebus attributum a Deo in quo bonum universi consistit.*[1]

God, therefore, has no need of the world. Since he is personal, he is free to create or not and free to create this world or another. The truth that God freely chose to create this world and freely chose to call us into existence is not merely an abstract philosophical doctrine but has an evident religious significance.

2

Since the world exists, we know that God did choose to create. A metaphysical difficulty presents itself, however, when we consider the place of the creative will in the being of God. God is infinite being and pure actuality, but, if he was free to create or not, is there not a potentiality in God which might not have been actualized? God is eternal and unchangeable, but, if he had not willed to create, might he not have been different from what he is? We must not, of course, suppose that the actual coming-to-be of the world makes any difference to the being of God. Although time had a beginning, the creative will of God is in itself eternal. The difficulty is not that God has changed, for this is plainly false; it is that God might in respect of creativity have been other than he is.

We find the answer once again in terms of being, when we consider whether the presence or absence of a creative will in God would add anything to the divine being or subtract anything from it. Whatever difficulties it may present to the

[1] St. Thomas Aquinas: *Summa Theologica*, I, qu. 25, ad. 3m.

imagination, the intellectual answer is evidently negative. The infinity of the divine being is not affected in any way by the presence or absence of a will to create. God is of himself infinite; his infinity of being covers a freedom to create or not and contains indifferently either the presence or the absence of a creative will; his actual will to create makes no difference to the infinity of his nature. This difficulty would be unanswerable in terms of mere essence; on this level the will to create appears as another item to be catalogued among the facts about God. The solution is to be found in the infinity of the divine existence, in relation to which such an item can be seen to make no addition.

The creation of the world, then, makes no difference at all to the divine being. The motive of creation must, therefore, be found in the absolutely free generosity of God, who wills that finite reflections of his infinite being should exist and have an actual share in the general nature of being. This, by a characteristic stroke of insight, was already affirmed by Plato.

Let us say why becoming and the universe were framed by him who framed them. He was good, and none that is good is ever subject to any notion of grudging. Being without grudging, then, he desired all things to become as like as might be to himself. This, teach the wise, is the true sovereign source of becoming and of the world.[1]

This is how we find in God a goodness analogous to freely chosen human goodness. Since degrees of being and degrees of value are correlative, God is essentially and necessarily, as infinite being, also the supreme value. Nothing can add to or subtract from this infinite goodness. But we can also find in the free creative act of divine generosity a kind of

[1] Plato: *Timaeus* 29E (A. E. Taylor's trans.).

goodness which is nearer our ordinary human conception of goodness.

Since God is supreme intelligence, his creative act involves a plan for the world which he creates. This casts a measure of philosophical light on the question whether the world had a beginning. Following St. Thomas we saw, in discussing the causal argument, that no metaphysical necessity demanded a beginning of the created world. The divine creative act is eternal, and the natures of things are capable of realization at any time; hence it was absolutely possible that God should have created a world with no beginning of its existence. But, if the things which make up the world are genuinely to have a history, a development and a fulfilment, it seems altogether appropriate that they should have had a beginning and should eventually reach a final and lasting state. Hence, while there is no metaphysical demonstration that the world had a beginning, there is at least a strong argument for the appropriateness of this to the creative intelligence.[1]

3

According to the different kinds of relation which created things and events bear to the divine will, the creative act itself is commonly differentiated as creation in a narrower sense, conservation and concurrence. Creation in the narrower sense is the calling of things into existence; conservation is their preservation in existence; concurrence is the communication of activity. It is evident that these things are not different on the side of God; they are aspects of his creative will which we distinguish in accordance with the different types of effect which it produces. The consideration of creation, conservation and concurrence suggests that we

[1] Cf. G. Rabeau: *Dieu, son Existence et sa Providence*, 1933, pp. 188–9.

should attempt a synthetic view of the divine causality and of the ways in which created causality shares in it. In the causal argument we rose from the thought of created causality to the first cause; now we can look back.

The divine causality is creative, being that of the absolute source of all finite being and becoming. Because it is eternal, it is not related differently to being and to becoming. In our way of thinking we make a distinction between creation and conservation as related to the being of things and between creation again and concurrence as related to their activity, but in reality the object of our thought is the one creative divine will. The divine causality, moreover, is purposeful in the fullest sense, having a complete prevision of all its consequences.

Created causality is not creative; it affects already existing things and makes them to become or be this or that but not to become or be absolutely. Where it is consciously purposeful, its foresight is limited. Since it is a causality of things which exist in duration, it is related differently to becoming and to being, and we have to distinguish between causes of becoming and causes of being. Created things possess potential natures which can be actualized in various ways; we must acknowledge within each thing itself an analogue of causality in the relationship of the substance or nature as agent to the attributes and activities which it has, in co-operation with circumstances, at this moment or at that. The proximate cause of being of the state of affairs at any moment must be found in the interrelated substantial natures of the things which exist. When we take duration into account, we find that the things which exist in their full actualization at any moment are the causes of becoming of the state of affairs which ensues. In the relatively super-ficial mode of causality which is the causation of becoming, we arrive at laws of becoming in terms rather of attributes than of substances; that is why the special sciences have comparatively little to say about substance. But causality is far from being merely a matter of becoming; we have to look also for causes of being, and, when we transcend causes of being this or that and recognize the necessity of looking for a cause of the absolute being of things, we find the causality of the infinite being who is God. ·

The divine causality is, therefore, the source of all other causality and combines all that is positive in other modes of causation. As creation in the narrow sense it is the source of the beginning of things; as conservation it keeps the world in existence; as concurrence it is the primal energy from which the active powers of all things are derived and pass into exercise. As an infinite and eternal act, the divine causality is equally related to every thing and event in the world and to every moment of the world's history.

The divine causality is so pervasive that it might seem that there was no need of created causality. Hence Geulincx and Malebranche developed the theory of occasionalism, according to which God is the sole real cause and the various states of created things provide no more than occasions upon which he exercises his prerogative as the source of being and becoming. This is half-way towards denying the reality of the world, and it is not surprising that a thinker as much influenced by Malebranche as Berkeley should in fact have denied the reality of material substance. The point is not that any complement of the divine causality is required but that, if finite things really exist, they have in their own order the causal powers which are inseparable from real being and reflect the divine causality without derogating from it.

On the other hand, a neglect to consider the divine exemplar of causation easily leads to difficulties about created causality. Hume, taking into account only finite causes of becoming, raised the difficulties about this specific kind of causation which haunt philosophy still. It is created causality which first leads us to envisage divine causality, but it is a final view of the various aspects of finite causality as imperfectly reflecting the fulness of divine causality that enables us to do justice to their degree of reality and to contemplate the causal order which characterizes the universe as a whole.

4

In the logical order which we have to follow in considering the various aspects of the simple and infinite divine being, God first knows his creatures as possible. Since they are possible beings, they reflect in different ways the being of God; hence God, by the infinite act of thought in which he knows himself, knows also all the possibilities of finite things. Here we may follow St. Thomas in making use of the Platonic language of ideas. The Platonic forms or ideas were the eternal exemplars in which the things of the world of experience participated and which were present to the mind of the Demiurge or World-craftsman when he shaped the world. On a fully theistic view the ideas cease to form a world of their own and become contents of the divine mind; moreover the divine knowledge is not merely of the universal natures of possible things but of every possible individual thing and of every detail about each. Since there is an infinite multitude of possible things, the single act of God's thought embraces this infinite multitude. All this follows clearly from the notion of an infinite being who is infinite intelligence.

In choosing to create those things which he actually creates, God knows them as existing. Since there can be no obstacle to the fulfilment of the divine will, it is the divine knowledge in conjunction with the divine choice which is the cause of the existence of the world. *Necesse est quod sua scientia sit causa rerum, secundum quod habet voluntatem coniunctam.*[1] God's being is eternal and entirely independent of time; hence his knowledge of the world is a simultaneous awareness of every detail of what for us is past, present and future. This knowledge of actual creation is given the name of knowledge of vision (*scientia visionis*), whereas the knowledge of the merely possible is described as the knowledge of simple intelligence (*scientia simplicis intelligentiae*).

Thus the whole created universe without limitation of time or space is present to God's mind, and God is present to it, in the knowledge of vision. It is in complete and continuous dependence on the divine power; hence God is present to it by his omnipotence. All created beings reflect in a finite way some aspect of the divine being; therefore God may also be said to be present to things by his essence. St. Thomas, then, sums up God's immanence in the world as being by essence, intellectual presence and power.[2]

While God is thus intimately present to the world, he transcends every finite thing and any collection of finite things by the infinity of his being, transcending time by an eternity which excludes duration by being more positive than duration and transcending space by an immensity which excludes extension by being more positive than extension. The erroneous identification of all reality with God which we call pantheism has had more than one motive and, consequently, more than one meaning. It has sometimes resulted from so overwhelming a realization of the divine infinity that finite things seem to be unreal; they are

---

[1] St. Thomas Aquinas: *Summa Theologica*, I, qu. 14, art. viii.
[2] St. Thomas Aquinas: *Summa Theologica*, I, qu. 8, art. iii.

dismissed as illusion or appearance, and we are urged to overcome the illusion or to penetrate through the appearance in order to sink ourselves in the one divine reality. This is to forget that finite being, although bearing no definable proportion to the divine being, is nevertheless being and, therefore, real in its own right.

Another form of pantheism is merely naturalism provided with a religious flavour by the description of the whole system of finite things as being necessary and divine. These two types of pantheistic attitude alternate elusively even in thinkers who employ similar modes of expression. It may be judged, for example, that there is more of naturalistic than of religious pantheism in Hegel and more of religious than of naturalistic pantheism in Bradley. Naturalistic pantheism, of course, is merely an undeclared variety of atheism. The remedy for both kinds of pantheism is a rational recognition, both of the experienced reality of finite things, and of the validity of the inference from them to infinite being; then we are able to preserve a right balance between the complementary truths of the divine immanence and the divine transcendence.

CHAPTER IX

GOD THE LAWGIVER

I

THE average contemporary scientist is not much worried about the metaphysical status of the generalizations at which he arrives. It used to be fairly commonly supposed that their validity depended on some ultimate principle of the uniformity of nature, but this turned out to be rather hard to define and still more difficult to establish within the frame of reference provided by modern philosophy. More recent researches into the logic of science have tended on the whole to suggest that we have little right to yield any strong measure of theoretical belief to the scientific conclusions which we nevertheless all accept in practice. The working scientist is not unduly perturbed; he is content with the pragmatic justification of his results which is every day available.

Yet anyone who looks for a complete philosophy can scarcely be satisfied with this state of affairs. A body of established and accepted conclusions whose theoretical justification remains obscure and ambiguous presents a genuine intellectual problem. This problem can only be solved within a wider frame of reference than modern philosophy provides. The difficulty has been caused by the modern neglect of metaphysics, and its solution is possible only through a science of being in general.

In the context of a religious philosophy the laws of nature have sometimes been regarded as expressions of the arbitrary will of God. This view is often attributed to William of Ockham; his real opinion seems to have been halfway towards it. He did not deny that things had their natural tendencies and, in a measure, their natural exigencies, but any or all of these could be nullified by the divine will. He thought, rather like Hume, that any two concrete elements of fact, since they could be conceived in isolation, could also exist in isolation. Hence an element of divine choice entered not only into the existence of things but into every case in which their natural relationships were actually verified. There could, then, be no certain deductive knowledge of the physical world; observation alone could tell us what relationships were always or usually verified. Thus Ockham reached a correct conclusion about the methods of physical science on a metaphysical basis which we must judge to be erroneous.

Since Berkeley denied the reality of material substance and attributed the regular and systematic character of sensible appearances, which show their independence of our minds, to their complete dependence on the mind and will of God, it is not surprising that he regarded the laws of nature as expressions of the divine will. Sensible appearances depending completely on God, God might conceivably have combined them in any arbitrary and chaotic fashion and might have presented different individual minds with entirely unrelated and unrelatable experiences. In fact, however, he combines them according to constant laws which are the same for all of us. Hence the physical sciences are possible, but they depend altogether upon the divine will, and Berkeley arrives at the picturesque conception of the laws of nature as being a kind of language by which God speaks to us and directs us.

The great Mover and Author of nature constantly explaineth Himself to the eyes of men by the sensible intervention of arbitrary signs, which have no similitude or connexion with the things signified; so as, by compounding and disposing them, to suggest and exhibit the endless variety of objects, differing in nature, time, and place; thereby informing and directing men how to act with respect to things distant and future, as well as near and present. [1]

We need not discuss Berkeley's immaterialism, but a comparison of his conclusion with his premisses serves to illustrate the truth that any approximation to this view of the laws of nature presupposes a diminished conception of the reality of finite things. A full recognition of the reality of created things involves the acknowledgment that, as they are, so they act; they have determinate natures with necessary properties. Consequently there are genuine laws governing their relationships, and a search for the laws of nature is legitimate. It does not follow that we shall arrive at a certain and exact knowledge of these laws. In reality the corporeal world has a kind of opacity to the human intellect which makes it necessary for us to employ the roundabout methods of induction, hypothesis and experiment. These methods lead in general to approximation and probability rather than to absolute precision and certainty. Nevertheless the whole search for a system of laws of nature would be misconceived unless there were laws of nature to be discovered. The need of the methods of observation is due not to any metaphysical deficiency in the reality of corporeal things but to their relative unintelligibility.

[1] Berkeley: *Alciphron*, Dialogue IV, § 12 (ed. Campbell Fraser, Vol. II, pp. 171–2.)

Hence, in a theistic context, St. Thomas sees the laws of nature not as expressions of the divine will but as reflections of the divine intellect. God, eternally contemplating the ideas of all possible things, contemplates also the laws of their natures and relationships. When we try to discover universal truths about the created world, we are trying to reflect with our minds aspects of an eternal divine truth. Here again, as in the case of causality, although this conception of an intelligible necessity in the laws of nature does not logically depend upon theism, a retreat from theism brings with it a tendency to obscure this metaphysical acknowledgment. This helps us to understand the divagations not of science itself but of the logical theory of science in modern times.

2

While the modern logic of science, as we have observed, has tended to make the theoretical justification of scientific generalizations highly problematic, their claims are often pressed to an inordinate extent when the subject of discussion is miracles. A miracle in a general sense is a direct divine intervention in the history of the created world; in a stricter sense it is a direct divine intervention in the corporeal sphere. In many circles it is difficult to induce people to take you seriously if you offer a defence of the miraculous. Yet, as a matter of philosophical truth, the possibility of the miraculous is directly entailed by theism. If there is no God, or if the divine is an impersonal force, there can, of course, be no such event as a miracle, but, if there is a personal God, it is patently inconsistent to deny the possibility of the miraculous.

Nevertheless, although an exclusive cultivation of the particular sciences at the expense of that general science of being which is metaphysics has in modern times obscured the logical basis of an investigation into the laws of nature, the reigning tendency since the rise of modern science in the seventeenth century has been to exalt impersonal law over personal will. The effect of mapping so much hitherto unexplored territory in detail has been an intoxication with the power of impersonal science. The admission of any originative capacity to personal will would seem to spoil the austere beauty of the newly revealed landscape. This remark has its application to human will as well as to the will of God.

It is not astonishing that Spinoza, for whom God and natural necessity are identical, should have denied the possibility of miracles. Nor is it surprising that Kant should have made a similar denial, since he regarded the regular application of the categories as a presupposition of any genuine experience. It is surprising, however, that so many ordinary theists should take for granted that miracles do not happen, since it is really so evident that God, who brought the world into existence in the first place, is no less capable of a direct intervention at any moment of its history.

A miracle, after all, is not the contradiction of a law of nature, nor is it precisely the suspension of natural law; it is rather the direct application of a higher power producing an effect of which natural agency is incapable. It is best conceived on the analogy of human will. The power to raise our arms at will does not contradict or suspend the law of gravity; it is the result of causality of a different order. So it is with the miraculous. Natural agency is incapable, for example, of the instantaneous restoration of decayed organic tissue, but God can obviously bring this about if he wills. No law of nature is contravened if the author of nature does what created things cannot do.

It must be admitted, therefore, that, given a personal God, miracles are possible. The question remains whether God would thus intervene in the course of nature. No miracle can be required in the sense that its result could not otherwise be attained, for this event might have been brought about in the ordinary course of providence. If, for example, someone is miraculously cured, divine providence might have seen that he never became ill, so that a miracle would not be needed. Hence, if miracles actually occur, it can only be because God wills them precisely as miracles, and that is as signs. The divine intention in a miracle must be that men should recognize his direct power exerted in it in order to bring some truth home to them. Miracles belong, consequently, to God's revelation of himself, and the discussion of their actual occurrence is a question of theology rather than of philosophy. But all the fantastic stories which have been concocted by human superstition and credulity, and which we rightly reject as having no historical foundation or religious significance, must not make us overlook the truth that the possibility of the miraculous is plainly entailed by theism.

3

The relationship of the moral law to God, since it is a law which may be followed or disobeyed, demands separate treatment. Many contemporary ethical thinkers, if they consider this relationship at all, take into account only the theory that moral obligation can be analysed in terms of the will of God. They ask whether the fact that I ought to do this means simply that God wills that I should do this. This theory, to which the school of William of Ockham inclined, but which is an unusual simplification of theistic ethics, can be refuted with ease.

We can always intelligibly ask why we ought to obey God, and the answer will be in terms of the goodness of the divine will. Hence we have still to ask how the divine will is good, and we are no nearer a definition of what moral obligation means.

When we have noticed this, can we proceed at once in the usual contemporary way to the opposite extreme and maintain that theism is irrelevant to ethics? It hardly seems so; there are other and less arbitrarily simplified theories of the relevance of theism to ethics. Besides, it can scarcely have escaped our observation that, in these days of less universal religious belief, the average man is content with a far more easygoing moral code than obtained in more religious periods of human history. It does not seem plausible to suppose that theism has nothing to do with ethics.

The serious question for theists is not whether moral obligation is fully analysable in terms of the will of God, which it obviously is not, or whether theism is irrelevant to ethics, which is equally unplausible, but precisely to what extent the existence of a good God as the creator of the world makes a difference to ethical facts. Thinkers who emphasize the importance of will, like Suarez, will say that, while the natural awareness of right and wrong is logically independent of a recognition of God, this does not amount to duty or obligation in the full sense until we apprehend the personal will of the creator enforcing this upon us. Others, like his contemporary Vazquez, will say that, although an acknowledgment of the relation of moral law to God makes a very real difference to the way in which the ethical imperative presents itself to us, the natural sense of right and wrong is already an awareness of moral obligation. In this respect Vazquez would appear to be more faithful to

St. Thomas, who insists always on law as an expression of reason rather than of will. In discussing the matter it is easy to lose oneself in verbal considerations about what moral obligation should be taken to mean; it will be more to the point if we ask what precisely is ethically knowable apart from God and what is added by a recognition of God.

It is evident that a moral agent does not have to take God explicitly into account in order to see what is right and wrong purely in respect of himself and of his fellow-men, for he has only to see what is appropriate to his nature and to the natures of the other persons and things affected by his actions. Ordinary human duties of self-development and self-discipline, and of justice and kindness to others, have a meaning for the atheist and the agnostic as they have for the theist. We need not accuse that now decaying type, once flourishing in the nineteenth century, the sternly ethical agnostic, of any lack of logical consistency in following his human moral code.

It does not follow, however, that even these purely human duties have exactly the same meaning for the atheist and the agnostic as they have for the theist. In the first place, as we have already remarked, an absolute code of morals points very directly to an eternal truth and an eternal mind contemplating it. When this consequence is denied or obscured, it is fatally easy to fall back on a notion of ethics as completely conditioned by human history and as evolving with it. T. H. Huxley, unconsciously living on an intellectual capital derived from theism, could affirm an absolute moral code and make clear how irrelevant evolution was to it; his grandson Julian Huxley, two generations later, is evidently incapable of understanding even what his grandfather meant, and of looking for an ethical standard elsewhere than in evolutionary history.[1] This aberration is not logically necessary, but it is psychologically only too natural.

The theist, therefore, is aware that his moral judgments, in so far as they are correct, reflect an eternal reality, which is the being and mind of God. Moreover, in the second place, he is aware that he is created. He is not an independent being belonging wholly to himself, nor is he merely a member of human society, but he belongs above all to God who made him. His moral duties are not simply duties to himself or to other men; they are duties to God who made the world and in whose plan for the world it is his privilege to co-operate. The reinforcement of moral consciousness which comes from a recognition of its real and eternal foundation is at the same time a reinforcement of moral duty, as owed to the eternal being upon whose absolute truth it is founded.

Furthermore, the theist knows that God wills that he should do what is ethically right. Here a distinction is needed; for what God in the full sense wills is infallibly fulfilled. Since the moral law is not infallibly fulfilled, it follows that, although God genuinely wills it, he does not will it in the full sense. The distinction is usually described as being between the antecedent and the consequent will of God. By his antecedent will God, perceiving what is good and what is demanded of human nature, prescribes it and puts it before men as the end of their activity. But God predominantly wills that men should be free and should freely co-operate with him. Hence, in the full sense, he wills consequently whatever follows from their choice, even if it deviates from the standard of right. The theist is aware

---

[1] Cf. the two Romanes Lectures of T. H. Huxley on " Evolution and Ethics" (1893) and of Julian Huxley on " Evolutionary Ethics " (1943), as contained in the volume *Evolution and Ethics* (1947).

of moral obligation as the object of the antecedent will of
God and, therefore, as a duty owed to the divine will as it
is owed to the divine reason. St. Thomas expresses this very
clearly when he speaks of the obligation of conformity with
the will of God.

The good which is present to the mind of God, who is
the creator and ruler of the universe, is the good of the
whole universe. Whence, whatever God wills he wills in
respect of the common good, which is his own goodness and
the good of the whole universe. Now a creature apprehends
by its nature some particular good proportionate to its nature.
. . . But no man rightly wills any particular good unless he
refers it to the common good as its end, just as the natural
tendency of any part is ordered to the common good of the
whole. Now the end provides, as it were, the formal ground
of willing what is referred to the end. Hence, in order that
anyone should rightly will any particular good, it is necessary
that, although what is materially willed is this particular good,
what is formally willed should be the common good and the
divine goodness. Therefore the human will is bound to
conform with the divine will in its formal object.[1]

The upshot of this is that a man, in willing what is right,
wills what in fact is the antecedent will of God. No human
act, right or wrong, is without objective reference to God;
there is no " philosophical " sin which is not " theological "
sin, or right action which is not objectively a homage to God.
A right act is objectively in conformity with divine reason
and divine will. In so far as a man understands this, he sees
the moral law not only as prescribing what is appropriate
to his nature and to the natures of the persons and things
affected by his actions, but as founded upon the eternal
mind of God and placed before him by the eternal will of

[1] St. Thomas Aquinas: *Summa Theologica*, Ia, IIae, qu. 19, art. x.

his Creator. There is an evident difference between what is simply an objective standard of right and wrong and what is a duty owed to the personal mind and will of the Creator. This is the difference between purely human morality and morality in a theistic context. Moral law is in reality the law of God, and it is fully understood as objective and absolute law when it is seen to be the law of God.

CHAPTER X

GOD AND FREE WILL

I

ACUTE controversy about the relationship of free will to God is still alive among philosophers who otherwise preserve a fair measure of agreement. The difficulties may be derived both from the divine omniscience and from the divine omnipotence. God's omniscience, however, does not present any very serious difficulty in this respect. The obscurity, such as it is, lies in God's complete knowledge of past, present and future. If God knows the future, people say, he knows what I will choose to do in the future. Does it not follow that I shall not really choose it freely but it must be already determined?

The error in this reasoning can be easily exposed. It consists in confusing the divine now with our now and, consequently, in supposing that God is aware of our future from the point of view of our now. If this were so, it would not be enough to say, as is sometimes said, that to know a fact and to determine it causally are not the same; hence God's knowledge of the future does not prejudice the free causation of our choices in the future. This would not be enough, for, if our future choices could be known from the point of view of our now, they would have to be already determinate, whether by a divine decree or in any other way. We can predict eclipses because the astronomical conditions now present are such that their eventual effects will determine an eclipse to occur. If the sun and moon freely decided when to have an eclipse, we could not predict eclipses.

The real solution is that God does not exist in time at all. His eternity is a simultaneous perfection of being which altogether transcends the distinction of past, present and future. God's point of view is an eternal now which is not our now. To it all times, past, present and future, are equally present. Hence God knows our future free acts simply as present in the now which, from our point of view, is not yet but will be theirs. This offers some difficulty to the imagination, but intellectually it is entirely clear.

Boethius had already arrived at this position, and it is the final theme of his work on the *Consolation of Philosophy*. He rests his answer to the difficulties about free will and the divine foreknowledge on the truth that to God belongs *semper aeternus ac praesentarius status*. Consequently the simplicity of the divine knowledge transcends the motion of time and has what for us is past as well as what for us is future present to it. It should be called rather *providentia* than *praevidentia*, rather providence than foreknowledge.[1] Boethius is certainly right in saying that to speak of God's foreknowledge is to speak inadequately, for, if the term were taken literally, it would imply that God existed in time and foresaw a future; really God's knowledge of everything is a wholly present knowledge.

St. Thomas employs in this connection the useful image of a man walking along a road and unaware of those who come after him, whereas someone who is looking down on the road from a height sees the whole succession of travellers at once at their different positions along the road. So we, at our point of time, have some knowledge of what is before us and are ignorant, except where inference from the

---

[1] Boethius: *De Consolatione Philosophiae*, V, pr. vi, 12–14.

present is possible, of what comes after us. God, on the other hand, looks down from his simultaneous eternity on the whole of time.[1]

The greatest imaginative difficulty about God's knowledge of what for us is future has no specific relation to free will, but it is convenient to mention it here. It is that the future is for us an indefinitely extended series of events, but God must be held to know it as a whole. There appears to be a contradiction in regarding an indefinite series as a closed totality. There would indeed be a contradiction if God were supposed to be aware of this series of events serially or one by one; in such a way it is evidently impossible to exhaust an infinite series. But, although God knows the series as a series, since it is a series, he does not know it serially or one by one; he knows it as a unity. There is really no more intellectual difficulty in understanding that God knows the infinite multitude of actual events, past, present and future, than in understanding that he is aware of the infinite multitude of possible things in the simplicity of his eternal act of thought. The imaginative difficulty, which we have to overcome, is the erroneous supposition that he knows actual events as we know them in a temporal series. He knows them as a temporal series, but he does not know them in a temporal series of acts of awareness.

2

We must devote rather more space to the difficulties which arise in respect of free will from the divine omnipotence. All reality is from God, and, since our human free acts are real, they are from God. Yet, if they are really free, they are in some ultimate sense from ourselves. Where do we

[1] St. Thomas Aquinas: *Summa Theologica*, I, qu. 14, art. xiii, ad 3m.

find the balance between these two truths? Two opposing views were formulated towards the end of the sixteenth century in the theories of physical premotion and of *scientia media*. The controversy was hot enough in its time, and, although it is now more peacefully conducted, it has by no means died out. Since both sides appealed to St. Thomas, we need not try to bring him into the battle. There is always the difficulty in appealing to a past thinker for the settlement of a later dispute that we cannot say how he might have explained his own statements if he had had the subject of the later dispute explicitly before him. Therefore we shall debate the rival arguments without invoking the patronage of St. Thomas.

The theory of physical premotion, as it is presented by Bañez and his followers, insists on the truth of the absolute divine omnipotence. All being and every element of being is from God. Hence our free acts are from God, not only in their results, but precisely in that real aspect of them which is their freedom. No created agent can pass into actual operation without the divine concurrence. Since this principle is absolutely general and applies to free agents as much as to others, we must hold that a human free act depends upon a divine premotion. This is called a physical premotion (*praemotio physica*), not in the modern sense in which physical is equivalent to corporeal, but in the ancient and etymologically more proper sense in which physical is distinguished from moral. God's influence upon our wills is not merely a presentation of motives which we might accept or reject; it is a genuine communication of being to our acts. God's omnipotence is such that he not only moves us infallibly to act in this way rather than in that, but he moves us infallibly to act freely in this way rather than in that; his causal efficacy extends to that mode of human action which is freedom.

How can we reconcile this divine premotion with the truth of human freedom and responsibility? In the last resort it is a mystery, but it is a mystery of the divine omnipotence, which is able to move us infallibly to choose freely; there is no way out of it by putting restrictions upon God's omnipotence. How can we thus explain sin without making God the author of it? The answer is that his premotion is towards the being of the sinful act, which, in so far as it is being, is good; its sinfulness consists in a deviation from right order which, as such, is negative and is to be attributed exclusively to the created will. The supporters of physical premotion assert both human responsibility and divine omnipotence to their fullest extent; they acknowledge a mystery but hold that we have no means of going farther. We must hold both truths and recognize that we cannot see how to reconcile them in the absence of a direct knowledge of God in himself.

The supporters of *scientia media*, from Molina onwards, have no objection to mystery; they know that the infinite being must be mysterious. Their objection to the doctrine of physical premotion is that it ends in contradiction rather than in mystery. To say that God moves us infallibly to act freely in this way rather than in that is not for them in the least mysterious; it is simply a contradiction in terms. Moreover it cannot be acquitted of making God as much the author of sin as he is the author of right actions. Hence the solution of the difficulty must be elsewhere.

The Molinist answer depends on this notion of *scientia media*, which is so called because it is halfway between the knowledge of simple intelligence and the knowledge of vision. By the knowledge of simple intelligence God knows everything that is possible; by the knowledge of vision he knows everything that he actually creates. But does not God know what any created will would choose in any circumstances in which it might be placed? In so far as this is a hypothetical fact, the divine knowledge of it is more than simple intelligence; in so far as it is hypothetical, it is less than vision. Hence such a knowledge may be described as *scientia media*. If God has this knowledge, he may call into existence precisely those wills whose choices will further his plan for the universe. Their choices will be free, but, since God eternally knows what they would be and freely calls them into actual existence, his omnipotence is in no way restricted. Here is a solution of the problem which involves no mystery that is really a contradiction and which does justice both to divine omnipotence and to human free will.

When two schools of thought, united in sound fundamentals, persist for centuries in contrary opinions on a particular question, it is fair to conjecture that neither is completely right and neither completely wrong. Any worthy judgment on the question must try to take into account what each side is legitimately insisting upon. Since the arguments for both opinions have been worked out again and again, and the contradiction still persists, we can scarcely hope to invent new reasoning; we can only indicate what premises and conclusions appear to us to be established and see what view appears in the end to be suggested.

3

In the first place we may ask whether the notion of *scientia media* can be upheld. Does it make sense to say that, apart from the actual existence of a created will, and apart from its actually being in the circumstances contemplated, it would certainly choose this rather than that? The opponents of Molina have often pointed out that this can scarcely be asserted without falling precisely into the determinism which Molina was concerned to avoid. Molina himself suggested that God had so perfect a knowledge of all possible finite wills that he could see exactly what they would choose under any possible conditions. We must agree with G. H. Joyce's comment that, " were this the true account of the matter it is difficult to see how the immediate agent could be really free."[1] If a perfect knowledge of the agent includes a knowledge of how he would act in any hypothetical case, he must be psychologically determined. If, on the other hand, the emphasis were transferred to the circumstances and it were held that a complete knowledge of the circumstances would entail a knowledge of the choice to be made in them, we have fallen into a circumstantial determinism. Joyce himself holds that we cannot throw any light on how *scientia media* arises, but asserts that we must accept it as a part of the divine knowledge of every possible order of things that God might create.

Thus *scientia media* appears in a naked light as an *ad hoc* hypothesis invented to reconcile free will with divine omnipotence. The attempt to avoid the mystery of the opposite school has landed us in another mystery, and we can hardly affirm that the mystery of *scientia media* avoids contradiction. For the whole character of a fully free act is that it has only existential determination. It is free precisely because it cannot be predicted from the nature of the agent and the circumstances. When the actual agent is placed in these actual circumstances, he actually chooses this rather than that, but, apart from the actual choice he makes in the order of real existence, he might indifferently have chosen this or that. Hence the statement that this possible free agent would in these possible circumstances

[1] G. H. Joyce: *Principles of Natural Theology* (ed. 2, 1924), p. 361.

choose this rather than that involves contradiction. We are trying to affirm freedom and determinism at the same time.

It has sometimes been asserted that the principle of contradiction or excluded middle itself enforces upon us the knowability of the propositions alleged to be contained in *scientia media*. If this possible free agent is placed in these possible circumstances, it is held that it must be true that the agent will choose this or not this. A little very elementary logic is sufficient to relieve us from this embarrassment. The contradictory of *If A, B* is not *If A, not-B* but *Not (If A, B) = A is compatible with either B or not-B*. If we are not compelled to assert that this possible free agent would in these possible circumstances choose this, we are not compelled to assert that he would not choose this; we can logically leave it as an entirely open question whether he would choose this or not. This is exactly what we must do in the case of a free choice. If *A* is the given will in the given circumstances and *B* is a possible choice, it is true neither that *If A, B* nor that *If A, not-B*. The truth that *Not (If A, B)* and *Not (If A, not-B)* means simply that *A is compatible with either B or not-B*. The solution of the question of fact can only be existential; it is only if an actual will is actually placed in these circumstances that it will actually choose either this or that.

The doctrine of *scientia media*, therefore, seems to involve the determinism which it was intended to avoid. It is not only a new hypothesis which no one had thought of propounding in a more absolute context and an *ad hoc* hypothesis which was invented to deal with a special difficulty, but it is an hypothesis which fails to solve the difficulty and lands its adherents in another difficulty of the same kind. We shall clear a part of the ground in this controverted question if we venture to affirm that *scientia media* lacks any adequate rational foundation.[1]

4

If the theory of *scientia media* does not commend itself to rational analysis and criticism, it in no way follows that its supporters were not trying to solve a genuine problem which the adherents of physical premotion had treated in too cavalier a manner. They were trying to give to moral responsibility a meaning which would be adequate to the whole deliverance of moral consciousness. The theory of physical premotion, applied without restriction, does not, indeed, seem to do justice to the facts of moral responsibility. Physical premotion is compatible with deliberate choice, but, if free choice never had any fuller meaning than deliberate

---

[1] It is sometimes held that, whether *scientia media* can be philosophically demonstrated or not, a divine knowledge of free futurables, i.e. of what individual wills would choose in given circumstances, must be admitted on theological grounds. The appeal is to certain scriptural passages, of which the two following are the most relevant. In 1 Kings Vulg. (= 1 Sam. A.V.) xxiii, David asks whether, if he remains in Ceila, Saul will come down and the men of Ceila will deliver him up. "And the Lord said: He will come down. . . . And the Lord said: They will deliver thee up " (vv. 11–12). The answers here may be perfectly well understood either of what was humanly likely or, more probably, of already formed intentions. In Luke x. 13 Christ says " Woe to thee, Corozain! Woe to thee, Bethsaida! For if in Tyre and Sidon had been wrought the mighty works that have been wrought in you, they would have done penance long ago, sitting in sackcloth and ashes " (Cf. Matt. xi. 21–3). This seems a quite natural way of saying that the dispositions of the people of Tyre and Sidon were such that they might have been expected to be more responsive than the towns in which Christ was preaching. In neither case can a certain divine knowledge of pure futurables be legitimately deduced. Therefore we agree with those theologians who hold, like L. Janssens, that God knows futurables which are really futurable in the sense either that they are contained with moral certainty in their causes or that God has decreed what they shall be; the other hypothetical propositions of this kind that we imagine for ourselves have no determinate truth-value but belong to the knowledge of simple intelligence, which is God's knowledge of the merely possible.

choice, we could scarcely have that sense of complete moral responsibility which we actually have. This general statement must be substantiated in detail.

The first and most crucial instance is the place of physical premotion in an act which is morally wrong. Here the Molinists are on their strongest ground and maintain with confidence that the doctrine of physical premotion makes God the author of sin. As we have already briefly noticed, they are answered by a distinction. God is the author of the entity of the wrong act, which, in so far as it is being, is good; the deviation from right moral order is essentially negative and must be attributed to the will of the creature. The Molinists retort that, while these aspects of the act are abstractly distinguishable, they belong concretely to one and the same fact: God cannot be conceived as positively willing the entity of the act without equivalently willing its moral wrongness. Their opponents are by no means unimpressed by this line of thought, and one of their answers makes a considerable difference to the theory. Garrigou-Lagrange, citing Billuart, holds that God does not move a created will towards the positive entity of a sinful act until the created will has itself fallen away from the right moral order. The negative deviation of the will logically precedes the positive divine premotion.[1]

While this answer satisfies the objection, it makes a considerable breach in the general principle upon which the doctrine of physical premotion is based. The divine causality is invoked only when the created will has made inevitable

---

[1] R. Garrigou-Lagrange: *Dieu* (ed. 4, 1923), p. 700, citing Billuart: *De Deo*, diss. viii, art. 5, ad. 3m: *Deus numquam determinat ad materiale peccati nisi creatura se prius quodam modo determinaverit ad formale. Quia Deus, ut provisor universalis, movet unumquemque secundum eius exigentiam et dispositionem, consequenter non movet ad actionem malam nisi voluntatem ex se dispositam et sic moveri exigentem.*

the direction in which it will be exercised. If the created will can thus deviate of itself from right moral order, it would seem that it can equally of itself embrace what is right. We are led, therefore, to examine the relationship of physical premotion to right action.

Let us suppose that we do not pursue this analogy, but apply the doctrine of physical premotion in its full rigour to right action. Then the divine causality infallibly moves the will both to desire what is right and to act in accordance with this desire. In what way, then, are we responsible for our right actions? They are ours, no doubt, in so far as they are deliberate; but neither the desire nor the consequent action could really, in the concrete, have been otherwise than as they are. The final choice is, consequently, an inevitable result of the deliberation because it is the fore-ordained result of the divine motion. We should be left with the conclusion that we are acting with full freedom only when we are acting wrongly. However defective we may be and are, this is surely a one-sided conclusion. If we are responsible for our wrongdoing, we must be allowed some share of responsibility for our right actions.

Yet, once again, the theory of physical premotion is insisting upon a truth which has to be taken into account and which tends to be overlooked on the opposite view. This is that no created agency can ever be an agency independent of God. However much the consciousness of moral responsibility may force us to stress the freedom of the created will, created will can never be so independent of God that it can make its choice in defiance of divine omnipotence. If God really and fully wills that anything should be, even if as the outcome of the decision of a created will, that thing will infallibly come to be. Whatever freedom we have is a freedom which God allows us, and he is always and in all circumstances capable of moving us to choose what he wills.

Therefore, if we begin from the human end, it seems that we must distinguish two senses of created freedom. The human will is radically free in so far as it proceeds from rational deliberation, which envisages good in general and is not fully satisfied by any finite good. But, just as in particular cases it cannot be reasonable, even on the results of human deliberation, to choose this rather than that, so God, if he wills, can in any particular case make it impossible in the concrete for us to choose this rather than that. Yet the consciousness of moral responsibility shows that we are sometimes free in a more complete sense. There must be instances of choice in which the outcome is dictated neither by the results of human deliberation nor by the overriding will of God. God, in his plan for our probation, provides us with occasions in which we are left with complete freedom of choice between ends presented to us. He need not do so, but he does do so. If he did not, our sense of moral responsibility would not be what it is. Hence, in trying to sum the question up, we shall have to satisfy both the complete efficacy of divine omnipotence and the reality of the freedom which divine omnipotence itself permits to us.

5

All being is from God. The creative act of God is not only a calling of things into being and a conservation in being but also a concurrence with the activity of creatures, without which they could not themselves give rise to new being. The activity of a free will needs the divine concurrence as much as any other kind of activity. A free will does not become, when once created, an agency independent of God; we must not conceive the relationship of a free will to God, with an anthropomorphism which becomes ridiculous when it is made explicit, as if God set it going and then had no further control over it. If God decrees that a created will shall choose this rather than that, such a choice will infallibly be made.

Moreover, this motion of God will not be an act of violence contrary to the nature of the will which is moved by him. God directs all things in accordance with their natures, necessary agents by strict causal laws and free agents according to their freedom. While God evidently could, by an exercise of omnipotence, cause a voluntary agent to act involuntarily in a particular case in the direction willed by God, this would, as an involuntary act, be outside our subject and, in any case, appears to contradict the principle that God directs things according to their natures. What bears on our present subject is that God may providentially direct that some end should be presented to a created will in such a way that the will cannot but choose to pursue it. This is no infringement of freedom in the general sense in which it refers to a choice made after rational deliberation, and its possibility is entailed by the general principle that all being is permanently dependent upon God.

Is it possible, however, that God should in this way make a wrong act inevitable? We must evidently answer in the negative, for the affirmative answer would clearly contradict the goodness of God. We must agree with Billuart and others that, in morally wrong action, the deviation of the will from right order logically precedes the divine co-operation with the positive activity in which this results. How, then, must we in this case conceive created freedom? It must be a freedom not only to choose after rational deliberation but a more absolute kind of freedom by which, even after rational deliberation, the will has the power to direct itself in this way or in that. If it chooses wrongly, the choice is its own, and God, who wills predominantly that his rational creatures should be responsible agents, co-operates with the positive entity of the action which follows.

But, in such a case, if the created will can choose wrongly, it can also choose rightly. If it really has this more absolute freedom of choice, it cannot be inevitable that it shall choose wrongly. Besides, if a wrong choice were inevitable in any case in which God did not make the right choice inevitable, God would be, at least negatively, the author of sin. Hence a created will is free in this more absolute sense to choose rightly, and God, who wills that we should be responsible agents, permits us this freedom to co-operate with him or to oppose him. We can be grateful, however, if he does not always leave us to this full freedom but sometimes directs us infallibly to the right by a motion which is not an infringement of freedom in the more general sense.

We must ask whether such a view of human freedom agrees with the divine omnipotence. There would be conflict only if human freedom were thought at any time to be out of divine control; this is a point on which the supporters of physical premotion rightly insisted. But it is always within the power of God to direct a created will infallibly. When God does not do so, and there is freedom of choice in the more absolute sense, it only enhances our sense of God's power that he should be able to create a free agent, to ask for its free co-operation, and to concur precisely with its free choice. If it were thought that, on this view, the divine plan for the world as a whole could be put out of joint by the action of creatures, this would be a singularly anthropomorphic objection. The divine wisdom must be evidently conceived as able to use the wrong choices of creatures as well as their right choices in order to forward the general plan of providence.

Finally, it must be asked how God knows such fully free choices. It has been objected that, apart from the doctrine of physical premotion, God is made dependent on his creatures for a part of his knowledge, for he will only know what they choose because they actually choose it. The general answer is that God knows it ultimately because he is God, and the divine nature is of itself omniscient; the final ground of the divine knowledge of free choices is, therefore, in the divine nature. It remains true, however, in another way, that God knows the choice because the creature makes it, and this objection, if it is an objection, can be brought against not only the opinion which we have expressed, but also the theory of *scientia media*, according to which God knows a choice because the creature will or would make it. The solution is parallel to the solution of the difficulty about God's freedom to create and his immutability. When, in the order of essence, we catalogue what seem to be the items of the divine knowledge, we find some in which he might seem to be dependent on his creatures. God, however, is not the all-embracing essence but infinite being. Just as the creative act adds nothing to his infinity of being, and just as its absence would subtract nothing from it, so God's knowledge of the free choices of created wills adds nothing to his infinite being. Creatures are not conferring being upon God, which would be absurd. It is because God is infinite being that he is omniscient and his infinite act of thought virtually contains all that is true, without any modification of its infinity arising from whether he chooses to create or not, or whether created wills choose in this way or in that. The mystery of God is always the mystery of infinite being.

These thoughts upon a much debated question are expressed positively but must be understood as offered for consideration rather than propounded as dogmas. It is something if we can see that the theory of physical premotion insisted rightly that a created will is never exempt from divine omnipotence, and that the theory of *scientia media* was nevertheless trying to solve a real problem and to do justice to our full sense of moral responsibility. These two exigencies must govern any attempt to throw light on the relationship of divine omnipotence and created free will.

CHAPTER XI

GOD AND EVIL

I

SINCE God, who is wise and good, created the world, its history must eventually unfold a plan which commends itself to reason and to moral judgment. Yet the nature and extent of the evil which is found in the world is such that to many minds it seems to contradict the conclusion and, therefore, also the premiss of our first sentence. Revulsion against evil is the one positive motive of atheism or agnosticism which deserves respect.

Some in the past have found a solution of the problem of evil in dualism, according to which the world is not the creation of a single God but a theatre of conflict between rival powers of good and evil. Such was the Zoroastrian theory, and such was the Manicheism which made such persistent reappearances in Western Europe from early in the Christian era until late in the Middle Ages. Dualism may, as in Manicheism, assert a somewhat unplausible opposition of mind to matter as good to evil. Yet the fact that no lively school or sect of dualists exists today need not prevent us from observing that, at a first glance, the general principle of dualism is not unplausible. The world does not look unlike a field of struggle between superhuman and independent forces of good and evil.

In more recent times, some attention has been given to the suggestion of William James, made especially in *A*

Pluralistic Universe, that God is finite, with limited wisdom and limited power, taking part in rather than governing the vicissitudes of history. We co-operate with God, and God co-operates with us, in pursuing the good of a universe which remains unfinished and only partly predictable for God as for us. This highly democratic theory of religion has a modest intellectual ancestry in the passing supposition of Cleanthes in Hume's *Dialogues concerning Natural Religion*, that the Author of Nature may be " finitely perfect " and exercise " benevolence, regulated by wisdom and limited by necessity ".[1] The same view is presented in J. S. Mill's *Essays on Religion* as an explanation of the mixed character of the world as it actually exists.

Intrinsically this theory seems rather less plausible than a dualism, in which there are two finite gods, each limited by the other and by the necessary laws of being, but where they are at least the supreme principle of good and the supreme principle of evil. In any case, since the existence of a single infinite good God is demonstrable, we do not have to refute either opinion directly. Nevertheless, the evils in the world are so striking, and sometimes so overwhelming, that we must consider how they can be reconciled with the existence of God. We cannot claim to present a solution which will be emotionally satisfying to all. A solution would perhaps be emotionally satisfying only if we could see positively how the evils in the world are made to fit into the plan of providence. But our knowledge of the world is far too limited in time and space for such a positive explanation to be possible. All that we can do is to show that the evils which exist are compatible with a God who is holy and omnipotent. This, since we know on other grounds that God exists, is intellectually sufficient.

---

[1] Hume: *Dialogues concerning Natural Religion*, part XI.

2

First, we must ask more exactly what evil is. The logical source of dualism was a persuasion that evil was real in the same sense as good. If there were wholly evil things as well as wholly good things, it seemed impossible to attribute them to the same origin. Evil is real enough, no doubt, and we are not going to be so foolish as to try to maintain that it is unreal. The negative doctrine of evil is not a theory that evil is unreal; it is an attempt to show that evil is real in a different sense from good.

The classical reference for the working out of the negative doctrine of evil is to the part of the *Confessions* of St. Augustine in which he describes how he battled his way out of Manichcistic dualism.[1] He tells how he gradually came to realize that everything that is, in so far as it is, is good; evil arises when things fall away from the degree of positive being which is due to them. The incorruptible being is the supreme good, but even corruptible things are good, for, if they were not fundamentally good, there would be nothing to be corrupted. So also moral evil is negative, since it is a perversion of the will from the right order appointed by the Creator.

Augustine's discussion is not an elaborate process of reasoning but a description of the slow growth of a simple acknowledgment. This method is correct, for it is a question of understanding what we mean by evil. Are we inclined to suppose, for example, that a venomous snake is evil? We have to realize that we call it an evil thing, not on account of what it is in itself, but on account of its possible effects on other living things. And these effects are evil because they injure or destroy life. Pain is evil, both because

[1] St. Augustine: *Confessions*, VII, 3–16.

it is an importunate sensation which hinders superior and more necessary activity and because it is a sign of a threat to life or health. Wrongdoing is evil, as far as the wrongdoer is concerned, because it diminishes and disintegrates his personality. Whenever we analyse an instance of evil, we find that its evil character, real as it is, resides in a negation of being.

Thus we see that being and good are correlative terms. Leibniz thought himself thereby justified in speaking of any negation of being as evil; in addition to physical and moral evil he introduced the conception of metaphysical evil (*malum metaphysicum*), which is any absence of perfection. In this sense, to be finite rather than infinite is metaphysically an evil. But this is an oversimplification of the relations of being and good and of not-being and evil. It cannot be reasonably said that it is evil for a man to be a man and not an angel, or for a dog to be a dog and not a man. This is no more reasonable than to say that it is evil for a man to have two eyes and not three. Good and evil have to be judged by a normal standard of structure and development. They presuppose that things have natures and potentialities which may be fulfilled or frustrated. Good resides in the positive fulfilment of the nature of a thing, and everything is good to the extent that, if its nature were not actualized in any degree, it would not exist at all. Evil resides in the frustration of the nature of a thing, in the privation of a kind of being and development which is due to it. Evil, then, is not simply negative but privative, presupposing a positive subject which lacks something that its nature demands.

When we understand that evil is not positive being but a privation of being, we do not have to ask why God creates evil or to seek its origin in a power independent of God. Only being is created, and being as such is good. We have still to ask, however, why God permits evil to affect the things that he creates.

3

We cannot, of course, say that God positively wills either physical or moral evil; he wills it only in so far as he permits it for the sake of a good which entails it. Therefore what we have to understand, in principle if not in detail, are the types of good for the sake of which God permits the various types of evil. If we can see as much as this, we shall have achieved our purpose.

To those who take free will seriously, moral evil does not present an insuperable difficulty. The power to make right free choices is also a power to make wrong free choices, and, if it is worth while that created free agents should exist for the sake of the special kind of created good which is attained by choosing rightly, wrong choices must be allowed. It may well be asked why God permits human wrongdoing to affect the innocent so constantly and often so disastrously, but it must be answered that moral responsibility for right as well as for wrong would be enormously diminished if the wrongdoer could hurt nobody but himself. It may again be asked why God created the human race at all if it was liable to behave as it actually has behaved, but it would be a mistake, even at a very evil period of history, to fall into too cynical a view of human nature. There are saints as well as sinners, after all, although the latter make more of an outward show.

The physical evil which worries us most is pain and suffering. If there were no moral evil, of course, the amount of human suffering in the world would be greatly reduced. Much suffering is directly due to moral evil, and, if the resources of human mind had been consistently applied to the relief of suffering instead of to less worthy objects, much of more natural suffering would have become avoidable. Yet, even if the human race had been perfect, there would have been no natural immunity from pain. Here we must, without exaggeration, take into account the value of suffering for the development of character both of the person who suffers and those around him. Without exaggeration, for it would be an intolerable hypocrisy to sing sublime praises of suffering while our shifts to avoid it so evidently show what we naturally think of it. Suffering is by no means always a help; it frequently brings out selfishness both in the sufferer and in others. Nevertheless we must admit, however reluctantly, that it has a real and important place in the development of human character, and we may not improbably estimate that, if moral evil and its effects were absent, the amount of natural suffering which would remain would be the right amount for this purpose. Even as it is, the saint can triumph over it and by means of it.

There is still the problem presented by pain in the animal world. We must, no doubt, resist the common tendency to anthropomorphize the feelings of animals; animal pain, being purely a matter of sensation and, in the case of more highly developed animals, imagination, is intrinsically less complete and also more transient than human suffering. But animals are not machines, and we cannot dismiss their sufferings as of no importance. Rights in the strict sense are the prerogative of rational agents in relation with other rational agents, but, while we cannot correctly speak of animals as having rights or of ourselves as owing duties to animals, we certainly have duties in respect of animals. Since pain is intrinsically evil, we are not justified in inflicting pain on any sentient creature except for the sake of some really greater good. Nor can we suppose that God is more indifferent to animal suffering than the more perceptive of his human creatures.

Nevertheless, when we reflect, we can see not obscurely that the sufferings which animals inflict on one another are the inevitable result of their natures. If animals are created at all, they will behave in the way that animals do behave. We can scarcely say that, on this account, animals are not worth creating. Doubtless God might have created, for example, only vegetarian animals, but he could not have created a vegetarian lion, for this is a contradiction in terms. It would be absurd to say in consequence that God should not have created the lion. Hence we must admit that the evils which we observe in the animal world are inevitable consequences of animal nature and are therefore permitted by the Creator.

Returning to human suffering, we must remark that it would scarcely be intelligible apart from immortality. If death were the end of everything, we might have some grudge against the Creator for having situated our short existence in so unsatisfactory a world. Those who find suffering an insuperable difficulty are usually to be found among those who do not believe in, or do not take seriously enough, the fact of immortality. When, on the other hand, we see the present life as a period of probation and preparation for something better, we are not overwhelmed by human suffering, but can divine its place in our phase of existence.

The evils in the world will always present a difficulty to the imagination, but they can be made acceptable at least to the intellect. Reflection shows that they are not incompatible with the existence of the wise, good and omnipotent God whom, on other grounds, we know to exist. We can see, in principle if not in detail, for what greater goods they are permitted. With our limited view of the great chains of cause and effect which make up history, we must be content with this degree of understanding and must wait for the fulfilment of the plan of providence, when God's wisdom and justice will be fully revealed.

CHAPTER XII

THEISM AND RELIGION

I

RELIGION in general is man's commerce with whatever he takes to be divine. If we are going to make this definition more precise, we shall have to determine what is meant by divine. Here two alternatives present themselves. The course adopted by most students of comparative religion is to take into consideration all the facts of history which might conceivably be described as religious and to try to find some highest common factor, which, not unnaturally, is pretty low. The inevitable result of trying to found a general notion of religion upon the whole mass of facts which might be called the religious history of mankind seems to be that religion itself becomes vaguer and vaguer.

For one who thinks that theism, the belief in a personal and creative God, is philosophically certain, another and more feasible alternative is available. He will take theistic religion as his standard of reference and attribute a religious significance to other human manifestations in so far as they bear an analogy to theistic religion. If theistic religion is religion in the full sense, he has a clearcut notion of what religion really is or ought to be, and can explore the bypaths without fear of losing the main road. The study of religion can be pursued with reference to a maximum rather than by an impoverishing attempt to discover a minimum.

From this point of view many of the facts which are studied in comparative religion will be judged as partial or complete aberrations rather than as positive attempts to arrive at a religious attitude. The mainspring of religion will always be, in spite of all the vagueness and all the mistakes of religious history, man's implicit apprehension that he owes his being to the infinite and eternal being who chose to create him. We shall be more interested in discovering traces of a recognition of this truth than in exposing the errors and inadequacies with which its formulation has been beset.

This has its application to the present as well as to the past. We can peacefully do justice to the various theories of the origin of religion which have been propounded by anthropologists, but doing justice to them will chiefly mean estimating the historical importance of wholly or partially mistaken applications of the religious impulse; in the same way we can see the religious impulse at work in contemporary forms which are not theistic, but we shall judge them with reference to theism. It would be a waste of time to try to isolate a faint generic quality which is common, say, to theism and pantheism; while we recognize the kinship, the difference is a great deal more important than the likeness. For it makes all the difference whether we worship something of which we are a part or some impersonal life-force in which we all share or, on the other hand, acknowledge ourselves to be wholly dependent upon a personal and transcendent God.

When we see ourselves neither as necessary in ourselves nor as parts of what is necessary; when we acknowledge that we have been called into existence by a personal being who alone is necessary; when we see ourselves thus as the effects of the free choice of infinite wisdom and goodness: then religion in the full and proper sense begins. If this is true, as theism holds it to be true, there is nothing slavish about such an acknowledgment. We really know ourselves in both our humility and our dignity when we see ourselves as wholly dependent upon, yet individually appointed by, the creative choice of God. In the discussion of religion, therefore, theism must provide the standard of judgment and interpretation.

2

The most important modern endeavour to analyse the fundamental religious attitude is to be found in Rudolf Otto's book on *Das Heilige* (*The Idea of the Holy*). It may seem strange that, in what purports to be a thoroughly intellectualistic treatment of religious truth, we should refer to a work which declares that it deals with *das Irrationale in der Idee des Göttlichen*. But *das Irrationale* is not here the irrational. In Otto's own view it is perhaps the non-rational; for ourselves, we think that it is better construed as the not explicitly rational. For religion is not a prerogative of intellectuals, and we can readily find expressions of true religion at a stage of thought which is far from being reflective and analytic. Otto's own rational schematism is the least satisfactory part of his book, but he has provided an admirable collection of sources for the understanding of what is fundamental to religion.

His celebrated and basic distinction of the *mysterium tremendum* and the *mysterium fascinans* is most completely expressed in a passage of St. Augustine. " What is that which shines through me and beats on my heart without injuring it? I tremble and I am on fire; I tremble in so far as I am unlike it, I am on fire in so far as I am like it."[1] God is at

---

[1] St. Augustine: *Confessions*, XI, 9. *Quid est illud quod interlucet mihi et percutit cor meum sine laesione? Et inhorresco et inardesco. Inhorresco inquantum dissimilis ei sum; inardesco inquantum similis ei sum.*

the same time a mystery of awe and a mystery of attraction. Both elements are present in all genuine religion. If the *mysterium tremendum* were all, there would be a service of fear which is not what we mean by religion; if the *mysterium fascinans* were all, a sentimental religiosity would result, which is equally far from religion.

On the one side religion is inseparable from a sense of our complete dependence upon God and our utter difference from him. The latter recognition gives rise to a sense of sin which is more fundamental than the sense of personal wrongdoing. Why otherwise do great saints think of themselves as sinners? It is not that they are conscious of any grave unfaithfulness to God; if they thought that they were great personal sinners, they would be exceptionally unintelligent saints. No doubt any minor unfaithfulness seems much worse to them than to the average man, but that is scarcely enough to account for the vehemence with which they acknowledge their sinfulness. What they really have is an enlarged sense of the distance which separates the creature from the Creator.

At the same time, if they are saints, they also have an enlarged sense of the divine attraction, of the *mysterium fascinans*. St. Augustine, in an even more familiar passage, speaks of God having made us for himself, so that our hearts are restless until they find rest in him. Our finite separateness and our continuous loss of ourselves in the passage of time are sources of anguish to the reflective mind, and even to the unreflective, until we find our wholeness again in relation to the Being who is infinite and eternal and who draws all things to a principle of unity. Since we were made by a personal being through an act of divine generosity, we must desire to know him and to follow the path which he lays down for us.

Among the manifestations of religion, Butler distinguishes four chief elements: " the institutional or external element of Church, sacraments, and public worship; the intellectual element of doctrine and dogma and theology; the mystical element of will and emotion and personal religious experience: and the element of service of others."[1] Logically the intellectual element comes first; we must know God before we can serve him. As human nature actually is, it is usually the institutional which mediates the intellectual to the extent that each individual can make it explicit. In any case, even apart from any revealed religion, we can see that human nature in its integrity will seek to progress beyond the merely abstract into a personal relationship, and that human nature as social will express its religion in social forms. Nor will religion be simply one of its various activities; all right action pertains to the service of God.

We said that human nature will desire more than an abstract knowledge of God; it will seek a personal relationship with him. But a personal relationship is not one-sided; if man seeks to commune with God, he will not succeed unless God wills to communicate himself to man. God's communication and revelation of himself to man is what we mean by the supernatural. Consequently a philosophical theory of the existence and nature of God and of man's attitude to God needs to be completed by an historical study of the way in which God communicates himself to man. This is theology in the strict sense, as distinguished from philosophy and even what is called natural theology.

[1] Cuthbert Butler: *Western Mysticism* (ed. 1, 1922), p. 292.

3

The possibility of the supernatural is the reason why treatises of natural theology patently tell only half the tale and why theories of natural religion are so obviously pale and inadequate. Natural theology could begin to arise among the Greeks because they were both endowed with speculative genius and extremely poorly provided with any substitute for a supernatural theology. We are inclined to blame Plato for his prosaic attitude of opposition to Greek religious myths because we think of the myths only as charming or curious poetic symbolism; he was opposed to the myths because he took them seriously as a ludicrously insufficient theology. He had, as best he could, to form worthy notions of God and of the soul, but he was aware that his speculations could not supply the place of an authentic divine word.

When Christian faith diminished, theories of natural theology and natural religion came to occupy the forefront once again. Herbert of Cherbury, in the first half of the seventeenth century, is the intellectual ancestor of many who thought that the essence of religion and Christianity itself could be reduced to a few truths which were rationally demonstrable and upon which all men could agree. John Toland, at the end of the century, with his *Christianity Not Mysterious,* is typical of those who forget that, if Christianity were not mysterious, it could scarcely be a religion, for God is certainly mysterious. This intellectual fashion has had its day, although it survives among some of the unreflective, who continue to identify with Christianity a few of the less exigent moral principles and a vague conception of God. For the reflective it is only too clear that a purely philosophical religion is much too fragile for survival.

Among Christians, however, a philosophical doctrine of God occupies a much less ambiguous place. For Christianity aims at being rational in a much fuller and more adventurous sense than any theory of natural religion; it offers a participation in the uncreated wisdom of God. If so, it will not be true to itself in neglecting the humanly rational; on the contrary, it must exhibit human reason in organic connection and harmony with the secrets of God. Hence St. Thomas and the other mediaeval masters rightly thought that they were all the more Christian for developing a doctrine of God as far as they could without invoking the support of supernatural faith. The contemporary Christian is not true to his tradition if he violently separates faith from reason, bases faith itself on irrational motives, and takes no interest in what human reason can tell us about God.

We claim, therefore, that right reason informs us of the existence of a personal God distinct from the world and originative of everything in it. On philosophical grounds alone we ought to acknowledge God and our fundamental duty to him. Beyond this we seek to enter into personal communication with him, but the actual fulfilment of this ulterior tendency, which is inchoate in our nature itself, depends upon an exercise of God's sovereign freedom. The fact belongs, therefore, to the sphere of the supernatural, and the doctrine of it will be a supernatural or revealed theology.